Classic
CLIMBING STORIES

Thirteen Awesome Adventures

EDITED *by*

KERRY L. BURNS

and

CAMERON M. BURNS

THE LYONS PRESS
GUILFORD, CONNECTICUT
AN IMPRINT OF THE GLOBE PEQUOT PRESS

The Lyons Press is an imprint of The Globe Pequot Press.

10   9   8   7   6   5   4   3   2   1

Printed in the United States of America

ISBN 1-59228-625-9

Library of Congress Cataloging-in-Publication Data is
available on file.

To Robert E. Robertson, with gratitude and respect, and, of course, thanks for sharing so many fine, if modest, misadventures.

Acknowledgments

This book would not have been possible without help from many people.

First, a huge thank you to Bridget Burke, director of the American Alpine Club Library in Golden. She answered dozens of questions, shipped oodles of boxes of books, and did all sorts of stuff a librarian should never have to do—and through it all she was extremely polite and helpful. Without her this book would never have come together.

Also, thanks for inspiration and ideas to: Peter and Sue Burns, Jill Murdoch, Pat and Gordon Webb, Heather and Rod Gough, Michael Burns and Jan Rumble, and Rob and Kian Murdoch.

Thanks also to our fellow adventurers: Ann, Zoe, and Mollie Burns; Mike, Penny, Jessie, Nattie, and Katie Sandy; Glenn, Gillian, Ryan, Kelsea, and Jamie Haste; Benny Bach, Angie Moquin, Charlie French, Amory Lovins, Stewie Oksenhorn, and Luke and Mel Laeser.

Last, but by no means least, a special thank you goes out to the two matriarchs of my (Cam's) family—Mary Burns and Sylvia Robertson—for wrangling small children while the menfolk wasted valuable time busting the spines and tearing out the pages of exceedingly rare and valuable AAC library books (kidding, Bridget!).

Contents

Introduction

Why does the activity of mountaineering produce so much literature? One of our climber friends, Steve Porcella, once described mountaineering as the single biggest producer of written works among all the sports and outdoors fields, and—whether that assessment is true or not—it's an activity that has certainly led to some of humankind's most fascinating literature. From straightforward narratives of ascents to meticulous self-examination to spiritual reveries, climbing prompts men and women to pour forth essays, articles, and books that are unlike any other field of literature.

And what makes a climbing tale a classic? That question would (and should) be answered differently by every mountaineer you might query. In our case, we wanted to showcase the amazingly vast spectrum that mountain-climbing literature offers—a sort of sampler pack, if you will. Who knows? One of these stories might spark your interest in European ascents of the Victorian Age, or a fascination with the development of climbing protection, or the role of women mountaineers through the ages, or even a renewed interest in mountains in your own backyard. This selection, we believe, covers the gamut of human experience, from joy to fear, happiness to desolation, and outstanding athletic and mechanical achievement to disaster.

Perhaps the earliest climbing story was Livy's description of the ascent of Mount Haemus in Thessaly (now known as Mt. Balkan in Bulgaria) by Philip of Macedon, the father of Alexander the Great, in the middle of the third century BC. He was engaged in war with the Romans and in the view from the summit hoped to discover the layout of the topography between the Adriatic and the Black Seas. Whether both oceans are visible or not, became the subject of an ancient controversy. When in 1836 Thomas Mitchell, the Australian explorer, saw Port Phillip Bay in Victoria from the mountains to the north, he compared his view to Philip's by naming his vantage points Mt. Macedon and Mt. Alexander. A second royal ascent was of Mt. Etna in Sicily by the Roman Emperor Hadrian, he of the northern British wall, in AD 121.

Then follows a long Dark Age in the story of mountaineering. It was broken by a flurry of mountain-adventuring stories at the beginning of the Renaissance. There was Petrarch, describing the ascent of Mount Ventoux near Avignon in 1336; the artist and naturalist Leonardo da Vinci climbed Monte Bo in 1511; the humanist Joachim Vardanius reached the summit of the Gnepfstein near Lucerne in 1518; and Konrad Gesner wrote lyrical words to nature after ascending Mt. Pilatus near Lucerne in 1555. Vardanius was a Swiss reformer, friend to Martin Luther, and supporter of Zwingli.

The first selection, "The Ascent of Mount Ventoux" by scholar and poet Francesco Petrarch, neatly bridges the archaic and Renaissance traditions. In 1336 he climbed the six-thousand-foot Mount Ventoux in Provence with three companions, including his brother. Petrarch has been named the founder of humanism, in which "people, not objective or absolutist factors, determine a thing's worth." He first compares the ascent to Philip of Macedon's royal ascent of Mt. Haemus nearly 1700 years before. His account then turns introspective and contemplates the spiritual, as in Gesner's writing, 200 years later. Many historians consider Petrarch the father of alpinism and his ascent the "birthday of alpinism."

Then followed another long hiatus, lasting over 200 years. Despite the naturalist and spiritual precedents of the early Renaissance pioneers and the bursting development of post-Renaissance art, science and industry, the mountains remained lonely haunts of primitive fears. This dark period was ending when Balmat and Paccard summited Mount Blanc in 1786. The lure of mineral collecting and high adventure had combined to open the mountains to a rapidly increasing group of mountain explorers.

Most major mountains around the world have seen their first ascents shrouded in competition, controversy, and post-ascent bitterness. The history of Europe's tallest mountain is no different. Jacques Balmat wrote nothing about this important 1786 climb, which he undertook with Dr. Michel Paccard, so the mountaineering community is indebted to T. Louis Oxley for recording the ascent and the subsequent search to find Balmat's resting place (recounted by Michael Carrier) in his 1881 story, "Jacques Balmat or The First Ascent of Mont Blanc: A True Story."

While the Balmats and Paccards of the late eighteenth century were rare animals, they were soon joined by more and more people who found stimulation in the heights. The third selection is by Henry David Thoreau, of Walden Pond fame. His ascent of Maine's Katahdin in 1846 is something of a "bridger of the gap"—that is, his ascent is at the far end of a period of little interest in mountain climbing, but, arguably at the front end of a massive explosion of interest in climbing mountains for pure sport.

Mountaineering blossomed through the late eighteenth and early nineteenth centuries, and in the mid-nineteenth century, the Victorian Age brought

British climbers *en masse,* and a great flourishing of the activity occurred. This was such an important age for mountaineering that we have included several selections from luminaries of the day, most of whose names won't ring any bells with today's gym rats and sport climbers.

Leslie Stephen's "The Schreckhorn" occurred in 1861 (it was Stephen who coined the term "the playground of Europe," which became the title of his 1895 book). Undoubtedly, the most prominent figure of this period of intense activity was Edward Whymper, whose 1865 first ascent of the Matterhorn and subsequent descent and disaster (as recorded in *Scrambles Amongst the Alps in the Years 1860–69)* are one of the greatest mountaineering stories ever written.

On the west side of the Atlantic, mountaineers of the mid- to-late-nineteenth century were not quite as common as they were in Europe, but it was a quickly growing activity. Some, like General Hazard Stevens, who in 1870 made the first ascent of Mount Rainier [Mount Takhoma], were still very much exploring the land; others, like Isabella Lucy Bird on Long's Peak in 1873, were being guided up now standard ascents. Stevens's factual account of Mount Rainier gives the modern climber some idea of just how difficult the Cascade terrain was, while Bird's "An Ascent of Long's Peak" from *A Lady's Life In The Rocky Mountains* is an endearing tale that proves that romance and mountain climbing have long coexisted.

Perhaps the most impressive climbing of that period was being done in the Canadian Rockies by people like James Outram, William Spotswood Green, Christian Kuaffman, and J. Norman Collie. Although we originally planned several pieces from this period, there is far too much fascinating literature from around the globe that we eventually narrowed it down to "Mount Assiniboine" by James Outram, who made the first ascent of this beautiful peak in 1901.

As the nineteenth century closed, several major trends were occurring globally with climbing. Alfred F. Mummery, who many consider the father of modern rock climbing, was exploring crack and face climbing techniques in the Alps. At the same time, Western climbers' attention was being more and more drawn to the greater ranges. Indeed, Mummery's attempts on Nanga Parbat (described here by J. Norman Collie) fit into a global "big range" pattern that included characters like Fresh-field, Conway, Purtscheller, Slingsby, Smythe, and the Duke of Abruzzi.

Into this mix of hardened pros we welcome Halford J. Mackinder, who was a bookwormish character with zero climbing experience and zero exploration experience. Yet, his story is amazing. After studying geology, biology, history, and law,

Mackinder was finally called to the bar in 1886. About the same time his law practice was becoming successful, Mackinder was invited by an officer of the Royal Geographic Society to put together his thoughts on geography. Mackinder became so engrossed in geography that every other intellectual or professional pursuit was quickly dropped. He quickly zeroed in on the 17,199-foot Mt. Kenya as an unclimbed opportunity and in 1899 miraculously managed to ascend it, proving just how inspirational mountains can be. To this day it is one of history's most amazing "off-the-couch"[1] mountaineering feats. (It's also interesting to note how Mackinder's detailed scientific observations early in the chapter are supplanted by his enthusiasm for the mountain world.)

One South American adventure is recounted: Annie Peck's 1908 first ascent of the north and lower peak of twin-summitted Huascarán, which she nevertheless titled "Victory at Last: The First Ascent of Huascarán."

Women seem to have been very active early on in mountaineering, so we rounded out the selection with another story from the fairer sex, mountaineer Freda du Faur's "The Ascent of Mount Cook," in which she describes a 1909 climb of New Zealand's tallest mountain.

The final story is one from our own Rocky Mountain backyard, the San Juans of Colorado. "First to Climb Lizard Head" by Albert L. Ellingwood is excerpted from the long-gone *Outing* magazine. Written in November 1921, it includes Ellingwood's colorful description of the geological history of the San Juans. Although Ellingwood's climbs are well known and very popular today (partly because they were so groundbreaking for the 1920s), one interesting thing about Ellingwood that gets little mention was his role in bringing fixed anchors to this country.

"Pitons made their way across the Atlantic to the United States in 1914 when Albert Ellingwood, an American who had climbed while in England, used them to protect a route later known as the Ellingwood Ledge on Greyrock in Garden of the Gods Park near Colorado Springs," noted Lloyd F. Athearn and Aaron J. Hill in a 2002 paper on fixed anchors. "Six years later, Ellingwood and partner Barton Hoag took their primitive metal spikes into the high peaks of the Colorado Rocky Mountains to protect their ascent of Lizard Head, a 13,113-foot rock formation, as well as to establish a fixed anchor from which they rappelled on the descent."

Ellingwood never authored an all-encompassing tome about his life and his climbs—most of his activities were written up as magazine pieces—so for climbers in the Rocky Mountain West, an ascent of Lizard Head is a fun, adventurous, not-too-hard must-do, and this essay sheds some light on Ellingwood and Hoag's impressive 1920 ascent.

We hope that readers find these stories as enjoyable as we did. They're all quite different, and yet they're all classics in their own way. Best of all, you can travel the world and get a lot of climbing done without ever leaving your living room.[2]

—*Kerry L. Burns and*
Cameron M. Burns, May 2005

---

[1] Although this term isn't quite the correct one for Mackinder's situation, it's close enough for our purposes.

[2] A quick mechanical note: many footnotes throughout these stories have been withdrawn from the original sources. Also, we tried to leave typographical idiosyncrasies as they appear in the original texts.

The Ascent
of Mount Ventoux

FRANCESCO PETRARCH

To-day I made the ascent of the highest mountain in this region, which is not improperly called Ventosum. My only motive was the wish to see what so great an elevation had to offer. I have had the expedition in mind for many years; for, as you know, I have lived in this region from infancy, having been cast here by that fate which determines the affairs of men. Consequently the mountain, which is visible from a great distance, was ever before my eyes, and I conceived the plan of some time doing what I have at last accomplished to-day. The idea took hold upon me with especial force when, in re-reading Livy's *History of Rome*, yesterday, I happened upon the place where Philip of Macedon, the same who waged war against the Romans, ascended Mount Haemus in Thessaly, from whose summit he was able, it is said, to see two seas, the Adriatic and the Euxine. Whether this be true or false I have not been able to determine, for the mountain is too far away, and writers disagree. Pomponius Mela, the cosmographer—not to mention others who have spoken of this occurrence—admits its truth without hesitation; Titus Livius, on the other hand, considers it false. I, assuredly, should not have left the question long in doubt, had that mountain been as easy to explore as this one. Let us leave this matter one side, however, and return to my mountain here,—it seems to me that a young man in private life may well be excused for attempting what an aged king could undertake without arousing criticism.

When I came to look about for a companion, I found, strangely enough, that hardly one among my friends seemed suitable, so rarely do we meet with just the right combination of personal tastes and characteristics, even among those who are dearest to us. This one was too apathetic, that one over-anxious; this one too slow, that one too hasty; one was too sad, another over-cheerful; one more simple, another more sagacious, than I desired. I feared this one's taciturnity and that one's loquacity. The heavy deliberation of some repelled me as much as the lean incapacity of others. I rejected those who were likely to irritate me by a cold want of interest, as well as those who might weary me by their excessive enthusiasm. Such defects, however grave, could be borne with at home, for charity suffereth all things, and friendship accepts any burden; but it is quite otherwise on a journey, where every weakness becomes much more serious. So, as I was bent upon pleasure and anxious that my enjoyment should be unalloyed, I looked about me with unusual care, balanced against one another the various characteristics of my friends, and without committing any breach of friendship I silently condemned every trait which might prove disagreeable on the way. And—would you believe it?—I finally turned homeward for aid, and proposed the ascent to my only brother, who is younger than I, and with whom you are well acquainted. He was delighted and gratified beyond measure by the thought of holding the place of a friend as well as of a brother.

At the time fixed we left the house, and by evening reached Malaucene, which lies at the foot of the mountain, to the north. Having rested there a day, we finally made the ascent this morning, with no companions except two servants; and a most difficult task it was. The mountain is a very steep and almost inaccessible mass of stony soil. But, as the poet has well said, "Remorseless toil conquers all." It was a long day, the air fine. We enjoyed the advantages of vigour of mind and strength and agility of body, and everything else essential to those engaged in such an undertaking and so had no other difficulties to face than those of the region itself. We found an old shepherd in one of the mountain dales, who tried, at great length, to dissuade us from the ascent, saying that some fifty years before he had, in the same ardour of youth, reached the summit, but had gotten for his pains nothing except fatigue and regret, and clothes and body torn by the rocks and briars. No one, so far as he or his companions knew, had ever tried the ascent before or after him. But his counsels increased rather than diminished our desire to proceed, since youth is suspicious of warnings. So the old man, finding that his efforts were in vain, went a little way with us, and pointed out a rough path among the rocks, uttering many admonitions, which he continued to send after us even after we had left him behind. Surrendering to him all such garments or other possessions as might prove burdensome to us, we made ready for the ascent, and started off at a good pace. But, as usually happens, fatigue quickly followed upon our excessive exertion, and we soon came to a halt at the top of a certain cliff. Upon starting on again we went more slowly, and I especially advanced along the rocky way with a more deliberate step. While my brother chose a direct path straight up the ridge, I weakly took an easier one which really descended. When I was called back, and the right road was shown me, I replied that I hoped to find a better way round on the other side, and that I did not mind going farther if the path were only less steep. This was just an excuse for my laziness; and when the others had already reached a considerable height I was still wandering in the valleys. I had failed to find an easier path, and had only increased the distance and difficulty of the ascent. At last I became disgusted with the intricate way I had chosen, and resolved to ascend without more ado. When I reached my brother, who, while waiting for me, had had ample opportunity for rest, I was tired and irritated. We walked along together for a time, but hardly had we passed the first spur when I forgot about the circuitous route which I had just tried, and took a lower one again. Once more I followed an easy, roundabout path through winding valleys, only to find myself soon in my old difficulty. I was simply trying to avoid the exertion of the ascent; but no human ingenuity can alter the nature of things, or cause anything to reach a height by going down. Suffice it to say that, much to my vexation and my brother's amusement, I made this same mistake three times or more during a few hours.

After being frequently misled in this way, I finally sat down in a valley and transferred my winged thoughts from things corporeal to the immaterial, addressing myself as follows:—"What thou hast repeatedly experienced to-day in the ascent of this mountain, happens to thee, as to many, in the journey toward the blessed life. But this is not so readily perceived by men, since the motions of the body are obvious and external while those of the soul are invisible and hidden. Yes, the life which we call blessed is to be sought for on a high eminence, and straight is the way that leads to it. Many, also, are the hills that lie between, and we must ascend, by a glorious stairway, from strength to strength. At the top is at once the end of our struggles and the goal for which we are bound. All wish to reach this goal, but, as Ovid says, 'To wish is little; we must long with the utmost eagerness to gain our end.' Thou certainly dost ardently desire, as well as simply wish, unless thou deceivest thyself in this matter, as in so many others. What, then, doth hold thee back? Nothing, assuredly, except that thou wouldst take a path which seems, at first thought, more easy, leading through low and worldly pleasures. But nevertheless in the end, after long wanderings, thou must perforce either climb the steeper path, under the burden of tasks foolishly deferred, to its blessed culmination, or lie down in the valley of thy sins, and (I shudder to think of it!), if the shadow of death overtake thee, spend an eternal night amid constant torments." These thoughts stimulated both body and mind in a wonderful degree for facing the difficulties which yet remained. Oh, that I might traverse in spirit that other road for which I long day and night, even as to-day I overcame material obstacles by my bodily exertions! And I know not why it should not be far easier, since the swift immortal soul can reach its goal in the twinkling of an eye, without passing through space, while my progress to-day was necessarily slow, dependent as I was upon a failing body weighed down by heavy members.

One peak of the mountain, the highest of all, the country people call "Sonny," why, I do not know, unless by antiphrasis, as I have sometimes suspected in other instances; for the peak in question would seem to be the father of all the surrounding ones. On its top is a little level place, and here we could at last rest our tired bodies.

Now, my father, since you have followed the thoughts that spurred me on in my ascent, listen to the rest of the story, and devote one hour, I pray you, to reviewing the experiences of my entire day. At first, owing to the unaccustomed quality of the air and the effect of the great sweep of view spread out before me, I stood like one dazed. I beheld the clouds under our feet, and what I had read of Athos and Olympus seemed less incredible as I myself witnessed the same things from a mountain of less fame. I turned my eyes toward Italy, whither my heart most inclined. The Alps, rugged and snow-capped, seemed to rise close by, although they were really at a great distance; the very same Alps through which that fierce enemy of the Roman name once made his way, bursting the rocks, if we may believe the report, by the application of vinegar. I sighed, I must confess, for the skies of Italy, which I beheld rather with my mind than with my eyes. An inexpressible longing came over me to see once more my friend and my country. At the same time I reproached myself for this double weakness, springing, as it did, from a soul not yet steeled to manly resistance. And yet there were excuses for both of these cravings, and a number of distinguished writers might be summoned to support me.

Then a new idea took possession of me, and I shifted my thoughts to a consideration of time rather than place. "To-day it is ten years since, having completed thy youthful studies, thou didst leave Bologna. Eternal God! In the name of immutable wisdom, think what alterations in thy character this intervening period has beheld! I pass over a thousand instances. I am not yet in a safe harbour where I can calmly recall past storms. The time may come when I can review in due order all the experiences of the past, saying with St. Augustine, 'I desire to recall my foul actions and the carnal corruption of my soul, not because I love them, but that I may the more love thee, O my God.' Much that is doubtful and evil still clings to me, but what I once loved, that I love no longer. And yet what am I saying? I still love it, but with shame, but with heaviness of heart. Now, at last, I have confessed the truth. So it is. I love, but love what I would not love, what I would that I might hate. Though loath to do so, though con-strained, though sad and sorrowing, still I do love, and I feel in my miserable self the truth of the well known words, 'I will hate if I can; if not, I will love against my will.' Three years have not yet passed since that perverse and wicked passion which had a firm grasp upon me and held undisputed sway in my heart began to discover a rebellious opponent, who was unwilling longer to yield obedience. These two adversaries have joined in close combat for the supremacy, and for a long time now a harassing and doubtful war has been waged in the field of my thoughts."

Thus I turned over the last ten years in my mind, and then, fixing my anxious gaze on the future, I asked myself, "If, perchance, thou shouldst prolong this uncertain life of thine for yet two lustres, and shouldst make an advance toward virtue proportionate to the distance to which thou hast departed from thine original infatuation during the past two years, since the new longing first encountered the old, couldst thou, on reaching thy fortieth year, face death, if not with complete assurance, at least with hopefulness, calmly dismissing from thy thoughts the residuum of life as it faded into old age?"

These and similar reflections occurred to me, my father. I rejoiced in my progress, mourned my weaknesses, and commiserated the universal instability of human conduct. I had well-nigh forgotten where I was and our object in coming; but at last I dismissed my anxieties, which were better suited to other surroundings, and resolved to look about me and see what we had come to see. The sinking sun and the lengthening shadows of the mountain were already warning us that the time was near at hand when we must go. As if suddenly wakened from sleep, I turned about and gazed toward the west. I was unable to discern the summits of the Pyrenees, which form the barrier between France and Spain; not because of any intervening obstacle that I know of but owing simply to the insufficiency of our mortal vision. But I could see with the utmost clearness, off to the right, the mountains of the region about Lyons, and to the left the bay of Marseilles and the waters that lash the shores of Aigues Mortes, altho' all these places were so distant that it would require a journey of several days to reach them. Under our very eyes flowed the Rhone.

While I was thus dividing my thoughts, now turning my attention to some terrestrial object that lay before me, now raising my soul, as I had done my body, to higher planes, it occurred to me to look into my copy of St. Augustine's *Confessions*, a gift that I owe to your love, and that I always have about me, in memory of both the author and the giver. I opened the compact little volume, small indeed in size, but of infinite charm, with the intention of reading whatever came to hand, for I could happen upon nothing that would be otherwise than edifying and devout. Now it chanced that the tenth book

presented itself. My brother, waiting to hear something of St. Augustine's from my lips, stood atten-
tively by. I call him, and God too, to witness that
where I first fixed my eyes it was written: "And men
go about to wonder at the heights of the mountains, and the mighty waves of the sea, and the wide
sweep of rivers, and the circuit of the ocean, and the
revolution of the stars, but themselves they consider
not." I was abashed, and, asking my brother (who
was anxious to hear more) not to annoy me, I
closed the book, angry with myself that I should
still be admiring earthly things who might long ago
have learned from even the pagan philosophers that
nothing is wonderful but the soul, which, when
great itself, finds nothing great outside itself. Then,
in truth, I was satisfied that I had seen enough of the
mountain; I turned my inward eye upon myself, and
from that time not a syllable fell from my lips until
we reached the bottom again. Those words had
given me occupation enough, for I could not
believe that it was by a mere accident that I happened upon them. What I had there read I believed
to be addressed to me and to no other, remembering
that St. Augustine had once suspected the same
thing in his own case, when, on opening the book
of the Apostle, as he himself tells us, the first words
that he saw there were, "Not in rioting and drunk-
enness, not in chambering and wantonness, not in
strife and envying. But put ye on the Lord Jesus

Christ, and make not provision for the flesh, to ful-
fil the lusts thereof."

The same thing happened earlier to St. Anthony,
when he was listening to the Gospel where it is written, "If thou wilt be perfect, go and sell that thou
hast, and give to the poor, and thou shalt have treasure
in heaven: and come and follow me." Believing this
scripture to have been read for his especial benefit, as
his biographer Athanasius says, he guided himself by
its aid to the Kingdom of Heaven. And as Anthony
on hearing these words waited for nothing more, and
as Augustine upon reading the Apostle's admonition
sought no farther, so I concluded my reading in the
few words which I have given. I thought in silence of
the lack of good counsel in us mortals, who neglect
what is noblest in ourselves, scatter our energies in all
directions, and waste ourselves in a vain show, because
we look about us for what is to be found only within.
I wondered at the natural nobility of our soul, save
when it debases itself of its own free will, and deserts
its original estate, turning what God has given it for
its honour into dishonour. How many times, think
you, did I turn back that day, to glance at the summit of the mountain which seemed scarcely a cubit
high compared with the range of human contemplation,—when it is not immersed in the foul mire of
earth? With every downward step I asked myself this:
If we are ready to endure so much sweat and labour
in order that we may bring our bodies a little nearer

heaven, how can a soul struggling toward God, up the steeps of human pride and human destiny, fear any cross or prison or sting of fortune? How few, I thought, but are diverted from their path by the fear of difficulties or the love of ease! How happy the lot of those few, if any such there be! It is of them, assuredly, that the poet was thinking, when he wrote:

Happy the man who is skilled to understand Nature's hid causes; who beneath his feet All terrors casts, and death's relentless doom, And the loud roar of greedy Acheron.

How earnestly should we strive, not to stand on mountain-tops, but to trample beneath us those appetites which spring from earthly impulses.

With no consciousness of the difficulties of the way, amidst these preoccupations which I have so frankly revealed, we came, long after dark, but with the full moon lending us its friendly light, to the little inn which we had left that morning before dawn. The time during which the servants have been occupied in preparing our supper, I have spent in a secluded part of the house, hurriedly jotting down these experiences on the spur of the moment, lest, in case my task were postponed, my mood should change on leaving the place, and so my interest in writing flag.

You will see, my dearest father, that I wish nothing to be concealed from you, for I am careful to describe to you not only my life in general but even my individual reflections. And I beseech you, in turn, to pray that these vague and wandering thoughts of mine may some time become firmly fixed, and, after having been vainly tossed about from one interest to another, may direct themselves at last toward the single, true, certain, and everlasting good.

Malaucene, April 26 [1336]

Jacques Balmat, or The First Ascent of Mont Blanc: A True Story

T. LOUIS OXLEY

Jacques Balmat was born in the village of Pèlerins, in the commune of Chamonix, in the year 1762. His fore-fathers had long been peasant proprietors, but his tastes differed from theirs; he was endowed with a vivid imagination and with invincible courage, and in order to increase the latter gift he constantly explored the surrounding mountains in search of minerals, for the science of which he had a perfect passion. His audacious courage had made him renowned even amongst his dauntless companions, and his ambition made him thirst to signalize himself by some memorable exploit. He therefore determined to gain the award which De Saussure had promised to the first man who should discover a path by which the summit of Mont Blanc could be reached. Numerous attempts had been made to attain this object, but hitherto without result.

Let us leave Jacques Balmat to relate his intrepid adventures in his own way, and with his quaint and naive preface to them.

"The determination to reach the summit of Mont Blanc was jogging in my brain night and day. During the day I used to ascend the Brevent, where I passed hours in trying to see a way to my coveted summit. I felt that I should live in a sort of purgatory if I did not succeed, and I could not resist this impulse to go to the Brevent. At night I had hardly closed my eyes when I dreamt that I was on my climb of discovery." . . . .

We will give but the last of his numerous dreams—it is too characteristic and too delicious to omit. In it he says: "I fixed my nails into the rock that they might act like cramps—I felt I was going to fall—I said to myself: 'Jacques Balmat my friend, if thou dost not catch hold of that branch above thy head, thine account will soon be settled.' The accursed branch could only be touched with the tips of my fingers—I raised myself up by my knees like a chimney sweep. Ah that branch! Now I clutched at it! I shall never forget that night! My wife awoke me with a great slap . . . imagine! . . . I was sticking fast to her ear all the time, and drawing it out as if it had been a piece of Indian rubber! After such an affair as this I said: 'Jacques Balmat you must now get the right sort of heart in earnest!' I thereupon got out of bed and put on my gaiters. 'Where art thou going?'

said my wife. 'In search of crystals,' I replied. I would not tell her what I was going to do. 'Do not thou be anxious if thou dost not see me this evening; if I have not returned by nine o'clock I shall sleep on the mountain.'

I took a strong stock with good iron points double the length and thickness of an ordinary one. I filled a gourd with eau-de-vie. I put a morsel of bread in my pocket, and away I started.

I had repeatedly tried to ascend by the 'Mer de glace' but the Mont Maudit had always barred my way. Then I used to return by the Aiguille du Goûté; but to ascend from there to the 'Dôme du Goûté there is an 'arête' (a backbone of rock) a quarter of a league long, and from one to two feet wide, and below a depth of 1,800 feet! This time I was resolved to try another route. I began by the one which leads to the mountain of the 'Côte;' after three hours ascent, I reached the glacier des Bossons: I crossed it—it was not difficult to do so; four hours later I was at the Grands Mulets—that was something. I had earned my breakfast. I ate a crust and drank off a cup. So far so good: but one had not then mounted so often to the Grands Mulets as to find a plateau—one was not quite at one's case there, I can assure you. At the end of two hours and a half of research I found a place bare of snow for about six or seven feet. It was here I determined to await the coming day—it was then about 7 o'clock. It was better to stay there than on the snow. I broke off my second crust and drank my second draught; then I installed myself on the rock where I was going to pass the night. It did not take me long to make my bed. Towards nine o'clock I saw a shadow rise from the valley like a thick smoke; it advanced slowly towards me. At half past nine it reached and enveloped me. Notwithstanding this shroud, I could see above me the last reflected rays of the setting sun which seemed loath to leave the highest point of Mont Blanc. But they did disappear—and with them the day. Turned as I was towards Chamonix; I had, on my left side the immense plain of snow which reaches to the Dôme du Goûté, and on my right—within reach of my hand—a precipice 800 feet deep: I dared not go to sleep for fear of falling outside my bed whilst dreaming. I sat on my bag and stamped my feet and clapped my hands incessantly to keep up the circulation. Soon the moon rose; pale, veiled in a circle of clouds: at eleven I saw a nasty mist cloud coming from the Aiguille de Goûté, which as soon as it reached me smacked me in the face with a dash of snow:—when I had covered my face with my handkerchief, I said 'Good! get along with you!' Every moment I heard the fall of avalanches which rolled down with a horrible rumbling sound like thunder. The glaciers cracked, and with every crack the mountain shook under me. Neither hungry nor thirsty was I, but I experienced a singular kind of headache, the pain beginning at the crown of the head and reaching to the eye-brows. The mist-fog continued; my breath became congealed on my handkerchief; the snow having penetrated through my clothes, I felt as if I were naked. I redoubled my movements and compelled myself to sing in order to drive away a heap of horrible ideas which began to haunt my mind. But my voice was lost in the snow: no echo answered to it: all was death-like in the midst of this frozen nature: and thus my voice had a strange effect upon me: I became afraid that I should commit suicide.

At last, at two o'clock, the sky began to whiten towards the east; I felt my courage returning as the sun arose and struggled with the clouds which shrouded Mont Blanc. I trusted that he would chase them away, but at four o'clock they became more dense; the effects of the sun becoming feebler, I came to the conclusion that it would be impossible to ascend further that day; but in order not to waste such an opportunity, I explored the neighbouring glaciers and passed the whole day in reconnoitering the best passages. As evening advanced and the mists followed, I descended to the Bec-à-l'oiseau, where night overtook me. I passed this one better than the last as I was not upon the ice and could sleep a little:—I awoke frozen through and through:—and it was only at the village of Moud that my clothes began to thaw.

I had gone about a hundred steps past the last houses in this village when I met François Paccard, Joseph Carrier, and Jean Michel Fournier—three guides. They had their bags and batons, and wore their climbing costume. I asked them where they were bound for—they replied that they were in search of some goats which they had given to the care of some shepherds—but, as these animals were not worth more than four francs each, this answer made me think that they wished to deceive me. I felt convinced that they were going to attempt the ascent, in which I had failed, and consequently to obtain the reward which De Saussure had promised to the first who should reach the summit of Mont Blanc. One or two questions which Piccard put to me about different points, and whether one could sleep at the Bec-à-l'oiseau confirmed me in my opinion. I replied that it was covered with snow, and that as a station it appeared to me un-advisable. I then saw him exchange a sign with the others, which I pretended not to notice; they retired apart and consulted together, and ended by proposing that we should all ascend together:—I accepted—but having promised my wife that I would not stay away more than three days, and not wishing to break my promise, I went home to tell her not to be uneasy, to change my stockings and gaiters, and to get some provisions.

At eleven o'clock at night I started again, without having been in bed; and at one o'clock I rejoined my comrades at the Bec-à-l'oiseau, four leagues below where I had slept the evening before. They were sleeping like marmots. I awoke them—in an instant they were all on their feet, and we all four set forward on our journey. This day we crossed the glacier of Tacconnay, and ascended as far as the Grands Mulets, where two nights before I had passed such hideous hours; then taking a course to the right, about three o'clock we reached the Dôme du Goûté. Already one of us, Piccard, was short of wind; a little above the Grands Mulets he had lain down, covered with the coat of one of his comrades. Arriving at last at the top of the Dôme we saw something black moving on the Aiguille du Goûté; we could not distinguish what it was; we could not tell whether it were a man or a chamois. We shouted out, and something answered us;—We remained silent awaiting a second cry; when these words reached us: "Ohé! "Halt! there are others who wish to ascend with you." We halted; and whilst waiting, Piccard, who had regained his wind, arrived.

At the end of half an hour the new comers joined us; they were Pierre Balmat and Marie Coultet, who had made a bet with others that they would reach the Dôme du Goûté before us. They had lost their bet. During this time, to utilize every moment, I went on a voyage of discovery. I clomb towards the Arête, now called the Bosse du Dromadaire, and got a quarter of a league nearer to the animal, on the aforesaid Arête.

Soon after I had quitted the others they had tried the same path, and had come to the conclusion that they were attempting the impossible. It was a rope-dancer's path—but that was all the same to me. I believe that I should have succeeded in reaching the end of it if it had not been cut in two with crevasses; besides the Arête was so sharp one could not walk upon it, so not wishing to have to return backwards and astride, I retraced my way to the place where I had left my comrades. I however found nothing but my bag—they had all gone!! At the sight of such temerity, and seeing that nothing would deter me, they left me, and quickly took the path with their backs towards Chamonix, supposing that I, being agile would soon catch them up. I found myself then alone, and for an instant I was as it were suspended between the wish to join them and the desire to attempt the ascent by myself. Their desertion had piqued me; something told me that I should succeed this time. I took up my bag and once more set off. It was now four in the afternoon. I crossed the Grand Plateau as far as the glacier of Brevna, from whence I could see Courmayeur and the valley D'Aosti in Piedmont. The mist was on the summit of Mont Blanc. I did not attempt to ascend, less from a fear that I should lose myself, than from a feeling of certainty that the others not seeing me on the summit would never believe that I had reached it. I took advantage of what remained of the day to seek a shelter, and spent an hour in vain in so doing; and, as I recollected that awful night—you know—I resolved to return home. I commenced my descent, but when I arrived at the Grand Plateau, not having provided myself with spectacles nor a green veil, the snow had so fatigued my eyes that I could see nothing. I had a kind of dazzling giddiness, which caused me to see great drops of blood. I sat down in order to restore myself; I let my head fall between my hands; at the end of half an hour my sight had come back, but the night had come with it; I had no time to lose. I arose to go, but had scarcely taken a hundred steps when I felt by my bâton that there was no depth of ice under my feet. I was at the edge of the great crevasse in which three guides had been lost. 'Ah!' I said to it, 'I know thee.' In fact in the morning we had crossed it by a bridge of ice covered with snow—this I tried to find; but the night was growing darker and darker, and my sight worse and worse. I could not find it. The pain in my head, of which I have spoken, again attacked me; I felt no desire to eat or drink; violent palpitations of the heart made me almost vomit. I must make up my mind to remain close to the crevasse until day break: to find the bridge of ice would take me another hour. I put down my bag on the snow; I made a curtain of my handkerchief, and did my best to prepare for such a night as before. Being 12,000 feet high, I must expect a much more intense cold. A fine needle-like snow froze me; I felt a languor and an irresistable desire to sleep; thoughts the most sad come across my mind, like unto those of death. I knew that these gloomy ideas and this longing for sleep were bad signs, and that if I had the misfortune to close my eyes in sleep, I should never open them again. From the place where I was I could see the lights of Chamonix where my comrades who had deserted me, were warming themselves by their firesides, or were comfortably in bed. 'Perhaps not one of them' (I said to myself) 'has given me a thought; or if one of them has thought of Balmat, he says, whilst rousing the embers of his fire, or pulling the coverlet more over his ears: "At this moment that imbecile of a Balmat is amusing himself by beating the soles of his boots together!" Keep up your courage, Balmat!' It was not that I wanted courage now, but strength. Man is not made of iron—and I felt that I was ill. In the short intervals of silence between the momentary falls of avalanches and the cracking of the glacier, I heard the barking of a dog in the village of Courmayeur, although the village was a league and a half from where I was. This noise took my thoughts away from myself; it was the only sound from the world below which reached me. Towards midnight the dog ceased to bark, and I fell back into that terrible silence which was like unto that of a churchyard:—for I took no account of the noise of the avalanches and of the glaciers, whose sounds frightened me. About two o'clock I saw the same white line, of which I have already spoken, dawn on the horizon; the sun followed it as before, and Mont Blanc had also put on his wig; and when he does that, he is in a bad humour and one must not provoke him. I know his character, and I think it right to let others know it too. As we say in the valley: 'When he smokes his pipe, one must not try to put it out.' At last when daybreak came, I was frozen; but by dint of friction, and practising the most absurd gymnastics, my limbs became more supple, and I was able to begin exploring once more. I had observed, when descending to the Grand Plateau, that half-way down there was an incline,—steep it is true—but everywhere accessible, and leading straight to the top of the Rochers Rouges, I decided to scale it; but found it so steep and the snow so hard that I could only hold on by making holes with the iron point of my stock; I succeeded in clinging to it, but I felt extreme fatigue and weariness. It was not an amusing thing to be suspended by one leg—so to speak—with an abyss under one; and to be obliged to cut the ice with the already blunted point of an Alpen stock. At length by force of patience and perseverance I gained les Rochers Rouges. 'Oh!' said I, 'from this spot to the summit there's nothing more to hinder you; all is joined together like one piece of ice!!' But I was again frozen through and through, and almost dead with hunger and thirst; it was late;—

I must descend—but this time with a certainty of succeeding during the first spell of propitious weather.

When I reached home I was almost blind. When my sight became somewhat restored I went (in order to avoid the flies) to lie down in the grange—and there I slept for 48 hours without waking.

Three weeks elapsed without bringing any favorable change in the weather, and without diminishing my ardour to make a third attempt. I imparted the secret of my discovery to Dr. Paccard, and associated him with my future intentions. It was agreed that we should start together the first fine day.

"At last on the 8th of August, 1786, the weather appeared sufficiently settled to hazard another trial. I went to Paccard and said to him 'Now Doctor, are you up to it? Have you any fear of snow; of ice; of precipices? Speak out like a man.' 'I have fear of naught when I am with thee, Balmat!' replied Paccard. 'Well then,' I said, 'the moment has come to creep upon la Taupinière.'

The Doctor said he was quite ready, but when he was about to shut his door, I think his courage began to fail him a little, for the key would not leave the lock—he turned it first one way and then another. 'Stay, Balmat' said he, 'we should do well to take two guides with us.' 'No,' I replied, 'I ascend with you alone, or you ascend with others. I wish to be the first, not the second.' He reflected for a moment,

then drew out the key, put it into his pocket, and followed me mechanically with bent head. In another
instant he pricked up his ears—'Ah well! I have confidence in thee, Balmat. Go on! For the rest, God's
mercy!' Then he began to sing, but not quite in
tune. This seemed to worry the Doctor. Whereupon
I took his arm, and said, 'This is not all Doctor; no
one must know of our project except our wives,' A
third person was however obliged to be taken into
our confidence: the shop-keeper of whom we
bought the syrup to mix with our eau-de-vie,
which, unmixed would have been too strong for
such an undertaking as ours. As this woman was
incredulous about what we told her, we invited her
to look the next morning at nine o'clock, towards
the side of the Dôme du Goûté. All our little matters
being settled, we bade adieu to our wives and
departed about five in the afternoon, one taking one
side of the Arve, and the other the other, so that no
one might suspect where we were going, and we
met again at the village of la Côtè or du Mont. I had
brought a coverlet, which served to enwrap the
Doctor as they swathe an infant. Thanks to this precaution he passed a good night; as for me, I slept
without waking until half past one. At two the white
line appeared; and soon the sun arose without a
cloud, without a mist, beautiful and brilliant, promising us a famous journey at last. In a quarter of an
hour's time we were engaged with the glacier of

Taconnaz, which we crossed without any accident, and soon we left the Grands Mulets below us. I showed the Doctor where I had spent the night: he made a significant grimace, and kept silence for some minutes—then stopping all at once. 'Dost thou think Balmat that we shall arrive to-day at the top of Mont Blanc?' I saw well what he was coming to—but I reassured him laughingly, without promising him anything. We went on for two hours and reached the Grand Plateau. The wind overtook us and became stronger and stronger. At length, after having scaled that well-remembered vertical barrier, we reached the rock of the Petits-Mulets. Here a gust of wind carried away the Doctor's hat, although it was tied on. Hearing his exclamation I turned round, and beheld his comfortable cap bounding down towards Courmayeur. He looked as if he were going after it with outstretched arms. 'Oh!' said I, 'we shall never see it again! It has gone into Piedmont; Bon voyage!' It seemed as if the wind took offence at this pleasantry, for scarcely had I shut my mouth when there came so violent a blast that we were obliged to lie flat on our faces in order not to follow the hat. We were not able to get up for ten minutes; the wind thrashed the mountains and passed whistling over our heads. The Doctor was discouraged. I only thought of the shop-keeper, who ought to be looking out for us at that moment to see if we were on the Dôme du Goûté. At the first respite which the 'bise' gave us, I got up; but the Doctor would only consent to follow on his hands and knees. In this way we pursued the course of a small mountain until we could see from it the village of Chamonix. Having gained this point, with my glasses I made out, 12,000 feet below us in the valley, our commercial friend with about fifty others, looking at us through their telescopes. A consideration for his amour propre made the Doctor get upon his legs;—The moment he stood up we saw that we were recognized—he, by his great coat, I by my usual clothes. The people in the valley saluted us with their hats; I replied with mine;—that of the Doctor was absent on an indefinite holiday. Paccard had spent all his energy in rising to his feet, and neither by the encouragements which he received from below, nor by those which I gave him, could he be induced to continue the ascent. After exhausting all my eloquence, and seeing I should only lose time, I told him to keep himself as warm as he could, and not to stand still. He listened without understanding me, and replied: "yes—yes" in order to get rid of me. I knew he must suffer from the cold; I myself was almost paralysed; I left him the bottle, and started off alone, telling him that I would come and fetch him. 'Yes—yes' he replied. I urged him again not to stand still, and off I went. I had not gone thirty paces when I returned, and found him, instead of moving about and stamping with his feet, sitting down, with his back to the glacial wind. This was at all events some precaution.

From this moment there was no great difficulty to encounter; but the higher I mounted the less respirable became the air: every ten steps I was obliged to stop like an asthmatic man; it seemed as if I had no lungs, and that my chest was empty. I tied my handkerchief round my mouth and breathed through it, and this relieved me a little. The cold had become almost insupportable: it took me an hour to walk a quarter of a league. Still I went on, with head bent down, until, all at once, coming to a point which I did not recognize. I lifted my head, and, lo! and behold!—at last, I had conquered Mont Blanc!

Then I cast my eyes around me—trembling lest I had deceived myself and I should find some aiguille, some new point which I had not the power to ascend; for the joints of my legs seemed to be kept in their places only by the aid of my trousers. No—I was at the end of so many explorings, so many unfruitful researches. I had reached the goal where no one had as yet been, not even the eagle nor the chamois; alone, I was here, without other aid than my will and my strength; all that surrounded me seemed to belong to me. It was four o'clock when I contemplated this giddy panorama; I looked down on Chamonix, I waved my hat, I saw through my glass that they replied by doing the same. All the village was on the 'Place.'

The first moment of exultation over, I thought of my poor Doctor. I descended as quickly as possible, calling out his name, and was terrified by not hearing him answer me; at the end of a quarter of an hour I saw him in the distance, round as a ball, but making no movement in spite of my shouts, which certainly must have reached him. I found him with his head between his knees, crouched like a cat when it makes itself into a muff. I took him by the shoulder; he raised his head mechanically. I told him that I had reached the summit of Mont Blanc; this news seemed to interest him in the most mediocre way, for in reply he asked where he could go to bed and to sleep. I rejoined that he had come to ascend Mont Blanc, and ascend it he should. I raised him up; I took him by the shoulders and made him walk some steps; he was as if drunk, and it appeared all the same to him whether he went to the one side or the other, up hill, or down hill. However, the exercise which I made him take restored his circulation a little, and he asked me if I had accidentally put into my pocket the hare-skin gloves which I had made expressly for my ascents, and which we call here 'mitaine' being without separation between the fingers. Situated as I then was, I would have refused them both to my own brother;—I gave him one of them.

At six o'clock I was once more on the summit of Mont Blanc, and my worthy Doctor too. Although the sun still shed bright rays of light, the sky was of a deep dark blue, and I could see the stars shining. Below us were ice, snow, rocks, pines; a panorama impossible to describe. I tried to make my Doctor a partaker of the extacy into which the spectacle which unfolded itself before our eyes had plunged me:—it was in vain; he saw nothing; the state in which he was had deprived him of his morale, and the effort to make him enjoy such contemplation was labour lost. As for me, I suffered no longer, I was no longer fatigued. I scarcely felt that difficulty of breathing which an hour ago had almost made me abandon my undertaking. In this state of rapture I remained on the summit for thirty minutes. It was seven o'clock—we had but two more hours of day-light—we must descend. I took hold of Paccard, I waved my hat as a last signal, and we began our downward journey. There was no track to direct us; the wind was so cold that even the surface of the snow was not melted; all we found was here and there on the ice the small holes which our stocks had made. Paccard was like a child, without energy or will; I guided him in the good parts, and carried him over the bad. Night began to fall whilst we crossed the crevasse at the foot of the Grand Plateau. It came upon us all at once. At each step Paccard stopped, declaring he would go no further; I made him go on, not by persuasion, which he no longer under-stood, but by sheer force. At eleven o'clock we left the regions of ice, and placed our feet on firm ground. It was more than three hours since we had lost all reflection from the sun; this being the case, I permitted Paccard to halt; and when preparing to wrap him again in the coverlet I found that he did not help me as before. On my remarking this to him, 'It is for the best of all reasons,' said he, 'I have no longer any use or feeling in my hands.' I drew off his gloves; his hands were as white as those of death. As for myself, the hand on which was the leather glove, in place of the hare-skin one, was in the same condition as his two. I said to him: 'Out of four hands, three are of no use.' This communication did not interest him; all he desired was to go to bed and sleep. But he said, 'Rub the frozen parts with snow; the remedy is not far to seek.' I began the operation with him, and ended it with myself; soon the circulation was restored, and with it the warmth, but with it pain as acute as if each vein were being pricked with needles. I rolled my baby in his swaddling clothes and lay down under the shelter of a rock; we ate a morsel and drank a cup, lay as close to each other as possible, and fell asleep. The next day at six, I was awoke by Paccard who said, 'It is droll, Balmat, I can hear the birds chirping and singing, and yet I cannot see the daylight; perhaps I cannot open my eyes; see if they have become like those of "a grand Duke."'[1] I told him that he was mistaken, that he ought to see. He then asked for some snow, which he melted in his hands and mixed with brandy, and applied to his eyelids—this operation was of no avail, it only made them smart the more. 'Balmat, I am blind!!' 'It seems very like it,' I replied. 'How am I to descend?' 'Take hold of the strap of my bag, and walk behind me. That is the way!' By this means we reached the village of Côte.

As I feared that my wife would be anxious, I left the Doctor, who felt his way home by tapping with his stock, and I returned to mine. When I beheld myself! I was not recognizable. I had red eyes, a black face, and blue lips; each time that I yawned or laughed the blood spirted from my lips:—in fact I was a spectre! . . .

Four days afterwards I set out for Geneva to announce the news to M. de Saussure—but some Englishmen had already preceded me in this mission."

We left Jacques at the moment when he was hastening to Geneva to announce to De Saussure the success of his enterprise.

We next hear of him, after the lapse of several years, in Paris, on a visit to Alexander Dumas pére, with whom he visited the museums, public buildings, etc. of the Capital. Being taken to see a Panorama of Chamounix and Mont Blanc, Balmat was so struck by the reality of the scene, that he burst into tears, and was seized with such intense "Mal-du-pays" that he was obliged to return immediately to his beloved valley.

The cultivation of Balmat's humble patrimony did not satisfy his ambition—he dreamed of riches—he many times engaged in commercial enterprises; hating restraint, he rarely undertook the office of guide, preferring hazardous, and more lucrative expeditions in search of minerals.

In September, 1834, giving credence to vague rumours, that there existed a rich vein of gold on the side of one of the high peaks which bound the valley of Sixt to the N. E., Jacques Balmat set out to discover it. He arrived near the spot indicated—to find it inaccessible. It was necessary to traverse a narrow ledge of rock, overhanging a frightful precipice—the sight of the danger daunted him, and for the moment he abandoned the attempt. Sometime afterwards, having obtained the assistance of an intrepid Chamois-hunter, he returned to the charge; and now in spite of the prayers and expostulations of his comrade, persisted—the fascination was too strong for him—he ventured upon the narrow ledge, took several steps, and—disappeared. The hunter, horrified, in despair, in a state bordering on distraction returned alone. No help could avail the unhappy Balmat; his death must have been instantaneous.

Picture to yourself a fall of more than 400 feet into an abyss covered with masses of rock, over which the avalanches swept continually, and you will have a faint idea of this horrible tomb.

At first the chief details of this melancholy accident were unknown at Chamounix; Balmat's companion hiding the truth, lest suspicion should rest upon him. Some shepherds of Sixt had also seen the unhappy man disappear, but kept silence from various reasons; the discovery of the precious mine being the main one.

The sons of Balmat made several fruitless attempts to recover their father's body. The information thee were able to acquire, respecting the scene of thy accident, was very meagre, and even had they had more reliable intelligence to go upon, they could never have succeeded in raising it out of the profound abyss.

Nineteen years rolled away without anyone thinking of undertaking fresh researches. The frightful description that was given of the abyss, at the bottom of which the unfortunate Balmat was lying, and the dangers that must be encountered, deterred the bravest hearts.

[2]"In September, 1853, some of our excellent guides, having had occasion to approach the spot whence Balmat had fallen, collected all the particulars they could about the place, and on their return to the valley of Sixt, where they had to conduct some travellers, they proposed to me (Michael Carrier) and others to make an expedition to discover, if possible, the remains of Balmat, in order to procure for them, Christian burial. The proposition was

received with enthusiasm; we set out, to the number of ten, for the valley of Sixt. The whole body of guides would, had it been necessary, have accompanied us, but we thought our party sufficiently numerous and capable; as, in its members, were united, courage, skill, and prudence.

We crossed the Brevent, descended into the valley of Diosaz, climbed the Col d' Anterne, and came down by the châlets of that name to the valley of Sixt.

After consulting two of the best guides of the place, and gaining all the information they could afford us respecting the passes and names of the localities we had to explore, we set off for the valley, from whence the only exit is by steep narrow chamois-tracks. Selecting one of these, about 3 miles and three quarters from the principal village of Sixt, our intrepid guides commenced a rapid ascent along the edge of the precipice; first they had to climb grassy slopes, alternating with almost perpendicular rocks, where they were obliged to make use of both hands and feet; then to cross several deep ravines, before arriving at the foot of a glacier surmounted by a wall of rock, from the height of which the eye could penetrate the dreadful abyss, which contained the remains of the first guide who had ever planted his adventurous foot on the top of Mont Blanc.

It was with sentiments of deep emotion that our guides regarded the frightful chasm, where Balmat had met so tragic a fate. Common prudence coun-selled them only to sound this gulf with their eyes, as, in addition to its horrible depth, every moment, avalanches of stones and ice engulfed themselves.

Auguste Balmat, one of the great nephews of Balmat, well known amongst the guides for his brav-ery, desired to be let down by a rope, and began the descent by the side, slipping every moment on the rotten schist which broke away under his feet. He had not gone far in this adventurous and daring enterprise, when he gave the signal agreed upon, to be drawn up and was received by his companions, and embraced by them, as they knelt on the last ledge of the precipice, as one does by an open grave. It was in truth an eternal tomb, consecrated by the fatal accident.

After having carefully identified the places desig-nated by the information collected the day before, and assured ourselves of the impossibility of pursu-ing more extended researches, we tore ourselves away from this horrible place and returned to Sixt, after having made a long detour, by the Glacier and the Pointe de Roant, as far as the Col-de-Chasse-roue.

"The next day, September 22nd, we passed by the Châlets of Sales to return to Chamounix.

However to convince ourselves that nothing had been neglected, and that the directions given were correct, we had a fresh and confidential interview with the Chamois-hunter who had accompanied Jacques Balmat on his last, and fatal expedition.

I had taken a sketch of the scene, which I put before him, whereupon he immediately recognised the various localities, and pointed out, without hesitation, the spot from whence Jacques Balmat had fallen."

So ends Michael Carrier's account.

What Michael Carrier had long wished was accomplished August 10th, 1878, when a Monument was erected to the memory of Jacques Balmat by the French Geograpicial Society, and placed in front of the Parish Church at Chamounix.

---

[1] A nocturnal bird of prey.

[2] Michael Carrier's account.

Mount Katahdin

HENRY DAVID THOREAU

B y six o'clock, having mounted our packs and a good blanketful of trout, ready dressed, and swung up such baggage and provision as we wished to leave behind, upon the tops of saplings, to be out of the reach of bears, we started for the summit of the mountain, distant, as Uncle George said the boatmen called it, about four miles, but as I judged, and as it proved, nearer fourteen. He had never been any nearer the mountain than this, and there was not the slightest trace of man to guide us farther in this direction. At first, pushing a few rods up the Aboljacknagesic, or "open-land stream," we fastened our batteau to a tree, and travelled up the north side, through burnt lands, now partially overgrown with young aspens, and other shrubbery; but soon, recrossing this stream, where it was about fifty or sixty feet wide, upon a jam of logs and rocks—

and you could cross it by this means almost any-where—we struck at once for the highest peak, over a mile or more of comparatively open land still, very gradually ascending the while. Here it fell to my lot, as the oldest mountain-climber, to take the lead. So, scanning the woody side of the mountain, which lay still at an indefinite distance, stretched out some seven or eight miles in length before us, we deter-mined to steer directly for the base of the highest peak, leaving a large slide, by which, as I have since learned, some of our predecessors ascended, on our left. This course would lead us parallel to a dark seam in the forest, which marked the bed of a tor-rent, and over a slight spur, which extended south-ward from the main mountain, from whose bare summit we could get an outlook over the country, and climb directly up the peak, which would then be close at hand. Seen from this point, a bare ridge at the extremity of the open land, Ktaadn presented a different aspect from any mountain I have seen, there being a greater proportion of naked rock rising abruptly from the forest; and we looked up at this blue barrier as if it were some fragment of a wall which anciently bounded the earth in that direction. Setting the compass for a northeast course, which was the bearing of the southern base of the highest peak, we were soon buried in the woods.

We soon began to meet with traces of bears and moose, and those of rabbits were everywhere visible.

The tracks of moose, more or less recent, to speak literally, covered every square rod on the sides of the mountain; and these animals are probably more numerous there now than ever before, being driven into this wilderness, from all sides, by the settlements. The track of a full-grown moose is like that of a cow, or larger, and of the young, like that of a calf. Sometimes we found ourselves travelling in faint paths, which they had made, like cow-paths in the woods, only far more indistinct, being rather openings, affording imperfect vistas through the dense underwood, than trodden paths; and everywhere the twigs had been browsed by them, clipt as smoothly as if by a knife. The bark of trees was stript up by them to the height of eight or nine feet, in long, narrow strips, an inch wide, still showing the distinct marks of their teeth. We expected nothing less than to meet a herd of them every moment, and our Nimrod held his shooting-iron in readiness; but we did not go out of our way to look for them, and, though numerous, they are so wary that the unskilful hunter might range the forest a long time before he could get sight of one. They are sometimes dangerous to encounter, and will not turn out for the hunter, but furiously rush upon him and trample him to death, unless he is lucky enough to avoid them by dodging round a tree. The largest are nearly as large as a horse, and weigh sometimes one thousand pounds; and it is said that they can step over a five-feet gate in their ordinary walk. They are described as exceedingly awkward-looking animals, with their long legs and short bodies, making a ludicrous figure when in full run, but making great headway nevertheless. It seemed a mystery to us how they could thread these woods, which it required all our suppleness to accomplish—climbing, stooping, and winding, alternately. They are said to drop their long and branching horns, which usually spread five or six feet, on their backs, and make their way easily by the weight of their bodies. Our boatmen said, but I know not with how much truth, that their horns are apt to be gnawed away by vermin while they sleep. Their flesh, which is more like beef than venison, is common in Bangor market.

We had proceeded on thus seven or eight miles, till about noon, with frequent pauses to refresh the weary ones, crossing a considerable mountain stream, which we conjectured to be Murch Brook, at whose mouth we had camped, all the time in woods, without having once seen the summit, and rising very gradually, when the boatmen, beginning to despair a little, and fearing that we were leaving the mountain on one side of us, for they had not entire faith in the compass, McCauslin climbed a tree, from the top of which he could see the peak, when it appeared that we had not swerved from a right line, the compass down below still ranging with his arm, which pointed to the summit. By the side of a cool mountain rill, amid the woods, where the water began to partake of the purity and transparency of the air, we stopped to cook some of our fishes, which we had brought thus far in order to save our hard bread and pork, in the use of which we had put ourselves on short allowance. We soon had a fire blazing, and stood around it, under the damp and sombre forest of firs and birches, each with a sharpened stick, three or four feet in length, upon which he had spitted his trout, or roach, previously well gashed and salted, our sticks radiating like the spokes of a wheel from one centre, and each crowding his particular fish into the most desirable exposure, not with the truest regard always to his neighbor's rights. Thus we regaled ourselves, drinking meanwhile at the spring, till one man's pack, at least, was considerably lightened, when we again took up our line of march.

At length we reached an elevation sufficiently bare to afford a view of the summit, still distant and blue, almost as if retreating from us. A torrent, which proved to be the same we had crossed, was seen tumbling down in front, literally from out of the clouds. But this glimpse at our whereabouts was soon lost, and we were buried in the woods again. The wood was chiefly yellow birch, spruce, fir, mountain-ash, or round-wood, as the Maine people call it, and moose-wood. It was the worst kind of travelling; sometimes like the densest scrub-oak patches with us. The cornel, or bunch-berries, were very abundant, as well as Solomon's seal and moose-berries. Blueberries were distributed along our whole route; and in one place the bushes were drooping with the weight of the fruit, still as fresh as ever. It was the 7th of September. Such patches afforded a grateful repast, and served to bait the tired party forward. When any lagged behind, the cry of "blue-berries" was most effectual to bring them up. Even at this elevation we passed through a moose-yard, formed by a large flat rock, four or five rods square, where they tread down the snow in winter. At length, fearing that if we held the direct course to the summit, we should not find any water near our camping-ground, we gradually swerved to the west, till, at four o'clock, we struck again the torrent which I have mentioned, and here, in view of the summit, the weary party decided to camp that night.

While my companions were seeking a suitable spot for this purpose, I improved the little daylight that was left, in climbing the mountain alone. We were in a deep and narrow ravine, sloping up to the clouds, at an angle of nearly forty-five degrees, and hemmed in by walls of rock, which were at first covered with low trees, then with impenetrable thickets of scraggy birches and spruce-trees, and with moss, but at last bare of all vegetation but lichens, and almost continually draped in clouds. Following up the course of the torrent which occupied this—and

I mean to lay some emphasis on this word *up*—pulling myself up by the side of perpendicular falls of twenty or thirty feet, by the roots of firs and birches, and then, perhaps, walking a level rod or two in the thin stream, for it took up the whole road, ascending by huge steps, as it were, a giant's stairway, down which a river flowed, I had soon cleared the trees, and paused on the successive shelves, to look back over the country. The torrent was from fifteen to thirty feet wide, without a tributary, and seemingly not diminishing in breadth as I advanced; but still it came rushing and roaring down, with a copious tide, over and amidst masses of bare rock, from the very clouds, as though a waterspout had just burst over the mountain. Leaving this at last, I began to work my way, scarcely less arduous than Satan's anciently through Chaos, up the nearest, though not the highest peak. At first scrambling on all fours over the tops of ancient black spruce-trees (*Abies nigra*), old as the flood, from two to ten or twelve feet in height, their tops flat and spreading, and their foliage blue, and nipt with cold, as if for centuries they had ceased growing upward against the bleak sky, the solid cold. I walked some good rods erect upon the tops of these trees, which were overgrown with moss and mountain-cranberries. It seemed that in the course of time they had filled up the intervals between the huge rocks, and the cold wind had uniformly levelled all over. Here the principle of vegetation was hard put to it. There was apparently a belt of this kind running quite round the mountain, though, perhaps, nowhere so remarkable as here. Once, slumping through, I looked down ten feet, into a dark and cavernous region, and saw the stem of a spruce, on whose top I stood, as on a mass of coarse basket-work, fully nine inches in diameter at the ground. These holes were bears' dens, and the bears were even then at home. This was the sort of garden I made my way *over*, for an eighth of a mile, at the risk, it is true, of treading on some of the plants, not seeing any path *through* it—certainly the most treacherous and porous country I ever travelled.

> "Nigh foundered on he fares,
> Treading the crude consistence, half on foot,
> Half flying."

But nothing could exceed the toughness of the twigs—not one snapped under my weight, for they had slowly grown. Having slumped, scrambled, rolled, bounced, and walked, by turns, over this scraggy country, I arrived upon a side-hill, or rather side-mountain, where rocks, gray, silent rocks, were the flocks and herds that pastured, chewing a rocky cud at sunset. They looked at me with hard gray eyes, without a bleat or a low. This brought me to the skirt of a cloud, and bounded my walk that night. But I had already seen that Maine country when I turned about, waving, flowing, rippling, down below.

When I returned to my companions, they had selected a camping-ground on the torrent's edge, and were resting on the ground; one was on the sick list, rolled in a blanket, on a damp shelf of rock. It was a savage and dreary scenery enough; so wildly rough, that they looked long to find a level and open space for the tent. We could not well camp higher, for want of fuel; and the trees here seemed so evergreen and sappy, that we almost doubted if they would acknowledge the influence of fire; but fire prevailed at last, and blazed here, too, like a good citizen of the world. Even at this height we met with frequent traces of moose, as well as of bears. As here was no cedar, we made our bed of coarser feathered spruce; but at any rate the feathers were plucked from the live tree. It was, perhaps, even a more grand and desolate place for a night's lodging than the summit would have been, being in the neighborhood of those wild trees, and of the torrent. Some more aerial and finer-spirited winds rushed and roared through the ravine all night, from time to time arousing our fire, and dispersing the embers about. It was as if we lay in the very nest of a young whirlwind. At midnight, one of my bedfellows, being startled in his dreams by the sudden blazing up to its top of a fir-tree, whose green boughs were dried by the heat, sprang up, with a cry, from his bed, thinking the world on fire, and drew the whole camp after him.

In the morning, after whetting our appetite on some raw pork, a wafer of hard bread, and a dipper of condensed cloud or waterspout, we all together began to make our way up the falls, which I have described; this time choosing the right hand, or highest peak, which was not the one I had approached before. But soon my companions were lost to my sight behind the mountain ridge in my rear, which still seemed ever retreating before me, and I climbed alone over huge rocks, loosely poised, a mile or more, still edging toward the clouds; for though the day was clear elsewhere, the summit was concealed by mist. The mountain seemed a vast aggregation of loose rocks, as if some time it had rained rocks, and they lay as they fell on the mountain sides, nowhere fairly at rest, but leaning on each other, all rocking-stones, with cavities between, but scarcely any soil or smoother shelf. They were the raw materials of a planet dropped from an unseen quarry, which the vast chemistry of nature would anon work up, or work down, into the smiling and verdant plains and valleys of earth. This was an undone extremity of the globe; as in lignite, we see coal in the process of formation.

At length I entered within the skirts of the cloud which seemed forever drifting over the summit, and yet would never be gone, but was generated out of that pure air as fast as it flowed away; and when, a quarter of a mile farther, I reached the summit of the ridge, which those who have seen in clearer weather say is about five miles long, and contains a thousand acres of table-land, I was deep within the hostile ranks of clouds, and all objects were obscured by them. Now the wind would blow me out a yard of clear sunlight, wherein I stood; then a gray, dawning light was all it could accomplish, the cloud-line ever rising and falling with the wind's intensity. Sometimes it seemed as if the summit would be cleared in a few moments, and smile in sunshine; but what was gained on one side was lost on another. It was like sitting in a chimney and waiting for the smoke to blow away. It was, in fact, a cloud-factory— these were the cloud-works, and the wind turned them off done from the cool, bare rocks. Occasionally, when the windy columns broke in to me, I caught sight of a dark, damp crag to the right or left; the mist driving ceaselessly between it and me. It reminded me of the creations of the old epic and dramatic poets, of Atlas, Vulcan, the Cyclops, and Prometheus. Such was Caucasus and the rock where Prometheus was bound. Æschylus had no doubt visited such scenery as this. It was vast, Titanic, and such as man never inhabits. Some part of the beholder, even some vital part, seems to escape through the loose grating of his ribs as he ascends. He is more lone than you can imagine. There is less of substantial thought and fair understanding in him, than in the plains where men inhabit. His reason is dispersed and shadowy, more thin and subtile, like the air. Vast, Titanic, inhuman Nature has got him at disadvantage, caught him alone, and pilfers him of some of his divine faculty. She does not smile on him as in the plains. She seems to say sternly, why came ye here before your time? This ground is not prepared for you. Is it not enough that I smile in the valleys? I have never made this soil for thy feet, this air for thy breathing, these rocks for thy neighbors. I cannot pity nor fondle thee here, but forever relentlessly drive thee hence to where I am kind. Why seek me where I have not called thee, and then complain because you find me but a stepmother? Shouldst thou freeze or starve, or shudder thy life away, here is no shrine, nor altar, nor any access to my ear.

> "Chaos and ancient Night, I come no spy
> With purpose to explore or to disturb
> The secrets of your realm, but . . .
> as my way
> Lies through your spacious empire up to light."

The tops of mountains are among the unfinished parts of the globe, whither it is a slight insult to the gods to climb and pry into their secrets, and try their effect on our humanity. Only daring and insolent men, perchance, go there. Simple races, as savages, do not climb mountains—their tops are sacred and mysterious tracts never visited by them. Pomola is always angry with those who climb to the summit of Ktaadn.

According to Jackson, who, in his capacity of geological surveyor of the State, has accurately measured it—the altitude of Ktaadn is 5,300 feet, or a little more than one mile above the level of the sea—and he adds, "It is then evidently the highest point in the State of Maine, and is the most abrupt granite mountain in New England." The peculiarities of that spacious table-land on which I was standing, as well as the remarkable semi-circular precipice or basin on the eastern side, were all concealed by the mist. I had brought my whole pack to the top, not knowing but I should have to make my descent to the river, and possibly to the settled portion of the State alone, and by some other route, and wishing to have a complete outfit with me. But at length, fearing that my companions would be anxious to reach the river before night, and knowing that the clouds might rest on the mountain for days, I was compelled to descend. Occasionally, as I came down, the wind would blow me a vista open, through which I could see the country eastward, boundless forests, and lakes, and streams, gleaming in the sun, some of them emptying into the East. There were also new mountains in sight in that direction. Now and then some small bird of the sparrow family would flit away before me, unable to command its course, like a fragment of the gray rock blown off by the wind.

I found my companions where I had left them, on the side of the peak, gathering the mountain cranberries, which filled every crevice between the rocks, together with blueberries, which had a spicier flavor the higher up they grew, but were not the less agreeable to our palates. When the country is settled, and roads are made, these cranberries will perhaps become an article of commerce. From this elevation, just on the skirts of the clouds, we could overlook the country, west and south, for a hundred miles. There it was, the State of Maine, which we had seen on the map, but not much like that— immeasurable forest for the sun to shine on, that eastern *stuff* we hear of in Massachusetts. No clearing, no house. It did not look as if a solitary traveller had cut so much as a walking-stick there. Countless lakes—Moosehead in the southwest, forty miles long by ten wide, like a gleaming silver platter at the end of the table; Chesuncook, eighteen long by three wide, without an island; Millinocket, on the south, with its hundred islands; and a hundred others without a name; and mountains also, whose names, for the most part, are known only to the Indians. The forest looked like a firm grass sward, and the effect of these lakes in its midst has been well compared, by one who has since visited this same spot, to that of a "mirror broken into a thousand fragments, and wildly scattered over the grass, reflecting the full blaze of the sun." It was a large farm for somebody, when cleared. According to the Gazetteer, which was printed before the boundary question was settled, this single Penobscot county, in which we were, was larger than the whole State of Vermont, with its fourteen counties; and this was only a part of the wild lands of Maine. We are concerned now, however, about natural, not political limits. We were about eighty miles, as the bird flies, from Bangor, or one hundred and fifteen, as we had rode, and walked, and paddled. We had to console ourselves with the reflection that this view was probably as good as that from the peak, as far as it went; and what were a mountain without its attendant clouds and mists? Like ourselves, neither Bailey nor Jackson had obtained a clear view from the summit.

Setting out on our return to the river, still at an early hour in the day, we decided to follow the course of the torrent, which we supposed to be Murch Brook, as long as it would not lead us too far out of our way. We thus travelled about four miles in the very torrent itself, continually crossing and recrossing it, leaping from rock to rock, and jumping with the stream down falls of seven or eight feet, or sometimes sliding down on our backs in a thin sheet of water. This ravine had been the scene of an extraordinary freshet in the spring, apparently accompanied by a slide from the mountain. It must have been filled with a stream of stones and water, at least twenty feet above the present level of the torrent. For a rod or two, on either side of its channel, the trees were barked and splintered up to their tops, the birches bent over, twisted, and sometimes finely split, like a stable-broom; some, a foot in diameter, snapped off, and whole clumps of trees bent over with the weight of rocks piled on them. In one place we noticed a rock, two or three feet in diameter, lodged nearly twenty feet high in the crotch of a tree. For the whole four miles, we saw but one rill emptying in, and the volume of water did not seem to be increased from the first. We travelled thus very rapidly with a downward impetus, and grew remarkably expert at leaping from rock to rock, for leap we must, and leap we did, whether there was any rock at the right distance or not. It was a pleasant picture when the foremost turned about and looked up the winding ravine, walled in with rocks and the green forest, to see, at intervals of a rod or two, a red-shirted or green-jacketed mountaineer against the white torrent, leaping down the channel with his pack on his back, or pausing upon a convenient rock in the midst of the torrent to mend a rent in his clothes, or unstrap the dipper at his belt to take a draught of the water. At one place we were startled by seeing, on a little sandy shelf by the side of the stream, the fresh print of a man's foot, and for a moment realized how Robinson Crusoe felt in a similar case; but at last we remembered that we had struck this stream on our way up, though we could not have told where, and one had descended into the ravine for a drink. The cool air above, and the continual bathing of our bodies in mountain water, alternate foot, sitz, douche, and plunge baths, made this walk exceedingly refreshing, and we had travelled only a mile or two, after leaving the torrent, before every thread of our clothes was as dry as usual, owing perhaps to a peculiar quality in the atmosphere.

After leaving the torrent, being in doubt about our course, Tom threw down his pack at the foot of the loftiest spruce tree at hand, and shinned up the bare trunk, some twenty feet, and then climbed through the green tower, lost to our sight, until he held the topmost spray in his hand. McCauslin, in his younger days, had marched through the wilderness with a body of troops, under General Somebody, and with one other man did all the scouting and spying service. The General's word was, "Throw down the top of that tree," and there was no tree in the Maine woods so high that it did not lose its top in such a case. I have heard a story of two men being lost once in these woods, nearer to the settlements than this, who climbed the loftiest pine they could find, some six feet in diameter at the ground, from whose top they discovered a solitary clearing and its smoke. When at this height, some two hundred feet from the ground, one of them became dizzy, and fainted in his companion's arms, and the latter had to accomplish the descent with him, alternately fainting and reviving, as best he could. To Tom we cried, Where away does the summit bear? where the burnt lands? The last he could only conjecture; he descried, however, a little meadow and pond, lying probably in our course, which we concluded to steer for. On reaching this secluded meadow, we found fresh tracks of moose on the shore of the pond, and the water was still unsettled as if they had fled before us. A little farther, in a dense thicket, we seemed to be still on their trail. It was a small meadow, of a few acres, on the mountain side, concealed by the forest, and perhaps never seen by a white man before, where one would think that the moose might browse and bathe, and rest in peace. Pursuing this course, we soon reached the open land, which went sloping down some miles toward the Penobscot.

The Schreckhorn

LESLIE STEPHEN

Most people, I imagine, have occasionally sympathised with the presumptuous gentleman who wished that he had been consulted at the creation of the world. It is painfully easy for a dweller in Bedfordshire or the Great Sahara to suggest material improvements in the form of the earth's surface. There are, however, two or three districts in which the architecture of nature displays so marvellous a fertility of design, and such exquisite powers of grouping the various elements of beauty, that the builders of the Parthenon or of the noblest Gothic cathedrals could scarcely have altered them for the better. Faults may of course be found with many of the details; a landscape gardener would throw in a lake here, there he would substitute a precipice for a gentle incline, and elsewhere he would crown a mountain by a more aspiring summit, or base it on a more imposing mass. Still I will venture to maintain that there are districts where it is captious to find fault; and foremost amongst them I should place the three best-known glacier systems of the Alps. Each of them is distinguished by characteristic beauties. The mighty dome of Mont Blanc, soaring high above the ranges of aiguilles, much as St. Paul's rises above the spires of the City churches, is perhaps the noblest of single mountain masses. The intricate labyrinths of ice and snow that spread westwards from Monte Rosa, amongst the high peaks of the Pennine range, are worthy of their central monument, the unrivalled obelisk of the Matterhorn. But neither Chamounix nor Zermatt, in my opinion, is equal in grandeur and originality of design to the Bernese Oberland. No earthly object that I have seen approaches in grandeur to the stupendous mountain wall whose battlements overhang in mid-air the villages of Lauterbrunnen and Grindelwald; the lower hills that rise beneath it, like the long Atlantic rollers beaten back from the granite cliffs on our western coast, are a most effective contrast to its stern magnificence; in the whole Alps there is no ice-stream to be compared to the noble Aletsch glacier, sweeping in one majestic curve from the crest of the ridge down to the forests of the Rhone valley; no mountains, not even the aiguilles of Mont Blanc, or the Matterhorn itself, can show a more graceful outline than the Eiger—that monster, as we may fancy, in the act of bounding from the earth;

and the Wetterhorn, with its huge basement of cliffs contrasted with the snowy cone that soars so lightly into the air above, seems to me to be a very master-piece in a singularly difficult style; but indeed every one of the seven familiar summits, whose very names stand alone in the Alps for poetical significance—the Maiden, the Monk, the Ogre, the Storm Pike, the Terror Pike, and the Dark Aar Pike—would each repay the most careful study of the youthful designer. Four of these, the Jungfrau, Mönch, Eiger, and Wetter-horn, stand like watchhouses on the edge of the cliffs. The Jungfrau was the second of the higher peaks to be climbed; its summit was reached in 1828, more than forty years after Saussure's first ascent of Mont Blanc. The others, together with the Finsteraarhorn and Aletsch-horn, had fallen before the zeal of Swiss, German, and English travellers; but in 1861 the Schreckhorn, the most savage and forbidding of all in its aspect, still frowned defiance upon all comers.

The Schreckhörner form a ridge of rocky peaks, forking into two ridges about its centre, the ground-plan of which may thus be compared to the letter Y. The foot of this Y represents the northern extremity, and is formed by the massive Mettenberg, whose broad faces of cliff divide the two glaciers at Grindelwald. Half-way along the stem rises the point called the Little Schreckhorn. The two chief summits rise close together at the point where the Y forks. The thicker of the two branches represents the black line of cliffs running down to the Abschwung; the thinner represents the range of the Strahlhörner, crossed by the Strahleck pass close to its origin. Mr. Anderson, in the first series of *Peaks and Passes*, describes an attempt to ascend the Schreckhorn, made by him under most unfavourable circumstances; one of his guides, amongst other misfortunes, being knocked down by a falling stone, whilst the whole party were nearly swept away by an avalanche. His courage, however, did not meet with the reward it fully deserved, as bad weather made it impossible for him to attempt more than the Little Schreckhorn, the summit of which he succeeded in reaching. A more successful attack had been made by MM. Desor and Escher von der Linth, in 1842. Starting from the Strahleck, they had climbed, with considerable difficulty, to a ridge leading apparently to the summit of the Schreckhorn. After following this for some distance, they were brought to a standstill by a sudden depression some ten or twelve feet in depth, which was succeeded by a very sharp arête of snow. Whilst they were hesitating what to do, one of the guides, in spite of a warning shriek from his companions, and without waiting for a rope, suddenly sprang down so as to alight astride of the ridge. They followed him more cautiously, and, animated to the task by a full view of the summit, forced their way slowly along a very narrow and dangerous arête. They reached the top at last triumphantly, and, looking round at the view, discovered, to their no small disgust, that to the north of them was another summit. They had indeed proved, by a trigonometrical observation, that that on which they stood was the highest; but in spite of trigonometry, the northern peak persisted in looking down on them. As it was cut off from them by a long and impracticable arête some three hundred yards (in my opinion, more) in length, they could do nothing but return, and obtain another trigonometrical observation. This time the northern peak came out twenty-seven metres (about eighty-eight feet) the higher. It was, apparently, the harder piece of work. Even big Ulrich Lauener (who, I must admit, is rather given to croaking) once said to me, it was like the Matterhorn, big above and little below, and he would have nothing to do with it. In 1861, however, the prestige of the mountains was rapidly declining. Many a noble peak, which a few years before had written itself inaccessible in all guide-books, hotel registers, and poetical descriptions of the Alps, had fallen an easy victim to the skill and courage of Swiss guides, and the ambition of their employers. In spite, therefore, of the supposed difficulties, I was strongly attracted by the charms of this last unconquered stronghold of the Oberland. Was there not some infinitesimal niche in history to be occupied by its successful assailant? The Schreckhorn will probably outlast even the British Constitution and the Thirty-nine Articles: so long as it lasts, and so long as Murray and Baedeker describe its wonders for the benefit of successive generations of tourists, its first conqueror may be carried down to posterity by clinging to its skirts. If ambition whispered some such nonsense to my ear, and if I did not reply that we are all destined to immortal fame so long as parish registers and the second column of the *Times* survives, I hope to be not too severely blamed. I was old enough to know better, it is true; but this happened some years ago, and since then I have had time to repent of many things.

Accordingly, on the night of August 13, 1861, I found myself the occupant of a small hole under a big rock near the northern foot of the Strahleck. Owing to bad diplomacy, I was encumbered with three guides—Peter and Christian Michel, and Christian Kaufmann—all of them good men, but one, if not two, too many. As the grey morning light gradually stole into our burrow, I woke up with a sense of lively impatience—not diminished, perhaps, by the fact that one side of me seemed to be permanently impressed with every knob in a singularly cross-grained bit of rock, and the other with every bone in Kaufmann's body. Swallowing a bit of bread, I declared myself ready. An early start is of course always desirable before a hard day's work, but it rises to be almost agreeable after a hard night's rest. This did not seem to be old Peter Michel's opinion. He is the very model of a short, thick, broad mountaineer, with the constitution of a piece of seasoned oak; a placid, not to say stolid, temper; and an illimitable appetite. He sat opposite me for some half-hour, calmly munching bread and cheese, and meat and butter, at four in the morning, on a frozen bit of turf, under a big stone, as if it were the most reasonable thing a man could do under the circumstances, and as though such things as the Schreckhorn and impatient tourists had no existence. A fortnight before, as I was told, he had calmly sat out all night, half-way up the Eiger, with a stream of freezing water trickling over him, accompanied by an unlucky German, whose feet received frost-bites on that occasion from which they were still in danger, while old Michel had not a chilblain.

And here let me make one remark, to save repetition in the following pages. I utterly repudiate the doctrine that Alpine travellers are or ought to be the heroes of Alpine adventures. The true way at least to describe all my Alpine ascents is that Michel or Anderegg or Lauener succeeded in performing a feat requiring skill, strength, and courage, the difficulty of which was much increased by the difficulty of taking with him his knapsack and his employer. If any passages in the succeeding pages convey the impression that I claim any credit except that of following better men than myself with decent ability, I disavow them in advance and do penance for them in my heart. Other travellers have been more independent: I speak for myself alone. Meanwhile I will only delay my narrative to denounce one other heresy—that, namely, which asserts that guides are a nuisance. Amongst the greatest of Alpine pleasures is that of learning to appreciate the capacities and cultivate the goodwill of a singularly intelligent and worthy class of men. I wish that all men of the same class, in England and elsewhere, were as independent, well-informed, and trustworthy as Swiss mountaineers! And now, having discharged my conscience, I turn to my story.

At last, about half-past four, we got deliberately under way. Our first two or three hours' work was easy enough. The two summits of the Schreckhorn form, as it were, the horns of a vast crescent of precipice which runs round a secondary glacier, on the eastern bank of the Grindelwald glacier. This glacier is skirted on the south by the ordinary Strahleck route. The cliffs above it are for the most part bare of snow and scored by deep trenches or gullies, the paths of avalanches, and of the still more terrible showers of stones which, in the later part of the day, may be seen every five minutes discharged down the flank of the mountain. I was very sanguine that we should reach the arête connecting the two peaks. I felt doubtful, however, whether we could pass along it to the summit, as it might be interrupted by some of those gaps which so nearly stopped Desor's party. Old Michel indeed had declared, on a reconnoitring expedition I had made with him the day before, that he believed, '*steif und fest,*' that we could get up. But as we climbed the glacier my faith in Michel and Co. began to sink, not from any failing in their skill as guides, but from the enormous appetites which they still chose to exhibit. Every driblet of water seemed to be inseparably connected in their minds with a drop of brandy, and every flat stone suggested an open-air picnic. Perhaps my impatience rather exaggerated their delinquencies in this direction; but it was not till past seven, when we had deposited the heavy part of our baggage and, to my delight, most of the provisions on a ledge near the foot of the rocks, that they fairly woke up, and settled to their task. From that time I had no more complaints to make. We soon got hard and steadily at work, climbing the rocks which form the southern bank of one of the deeply-carved gullies of which I have spoken. It seemed clear to me that the summit of the Schreck-horn, which was invisible to us at present, was on the other side of this ravine, its northern bank being in fact formed by a huge buttress running straight down from the peak. This buttress was cut into steps, by cliffs so steep as to be perfectly impracticable; in fact, I believe that in one place it absolutely overhung. It was therefore necessary to keep to the other side; but I felt an unpleasant suspicion that the head of the ravine might correspond with an impracticable gap in the arête.

Meanwhile we had simply a steady piece of rock-climbing. Christian Michel, a first-rate cragsman, led the way. Kaufmann followed, and, as we clung to the crannies and ledges of the rock, relieved his mind by sundry sarcasms as to the length of arm and leg which enabled me to reach points of support without putting my limbs out of joint—an advantage, to say the truth, which he could well afford to give away. The rocks were steep and slippery, and occasionally covered with a coat of ice. We were frequently flattened out against the rocks, like beasts of ill-repute nailed to a barn, with fingers and toes inserted into four different cracks which tested the elasticity of our frames to the uttermost. Still our progress though slow was steady, and would have been agreeable if only our minds could have been at ease with regard to that detestable ravine. We could not obtain a glimpse of the final ridge, and we might be hopelessly stopped at the last step. Meanwhile, as we looked round, we could see the glacier basins gradually sinking, and the sharp pyramid of the Finsteraarhorn shooting upwards above them. Gradually, too, the distant ranges of Alps climbed higher and higher up the southern horizon. From Mont Blanc to Monte Rosa, and away to the distant Bernina, ridge beyond ridge rose into the sky, with many a well-remembered old friend amongst them. In two or three hours' work we had risen high enough to look over the ridge connecting the two peaks, down the long reaches of the Aar glaciers. A few minutes afterwards we caught sight of a row of black dots creeping over the snows of the Strahleck. With a telescope I could just distinguish a friend whom I had met the day before at Grindelwald. A loud shout from us brought back a faint reply or echo. We were already high above the pass. Still, however, that last arête remained pertinaciously invisible. A few more steps, if "steps" is a word applicable to progression by hands as well as feet, placed us at last on the great ridge of the mountain, looking down upon the Lauteraar Sattel. But the ridge rose between us and the peak into a kind of knob, which allowed only a few yards of it to be visible. The present route, as I believe, leads to the ridge at the point further from the summit of the mountain. We were, however, near the point where a late melancholy accident will, it is to be hoped, impress upon future travellers the necessity for a scrupulous adherence to all recognised precautions. The scene was in itself significant enough for men of weak nerves. Taking a drop of brandy all round, we turned to the assault, feeling that a few yards more would decide the question. On our right hand the long slopes of snow ran down towards the Lauteraar Sattel, as straight as if the long furrows on their surface had been drawn by a ruler. They were in a most ticklish state. The snow seemed to be piled up like loose sand, at the highest angle of rest, and almost without cohesion. The fall of a pebble or a handful of snow was sufficient to detach a layer, which slid smoothly down the long slopes with a low ominous hiss. Clinging, however, to the rocks which formed the crest of the ridge, we dug our feet as far as possible into the older snow beneath, and crept cautiously along. As soon as there was room on the arête, we took to the rocks again, and began with breathless expectation climbing the knob of which I have spoken. The top of the mountain could not remain much longer concealed. A few yards more, and it came full in view. The next step revealed to me not only the mountain top, but a lovely and almost level ridge which connected it with our standing-point. We had won the victory, and, with a sense of intense satisfaction, attacked the short ridge which still divided us from our object. It is melancholy to observe the shockingly bad state of repair of the higher peaks, and the present was no exception to the rule. Loose stones rattled down the mountain sides at every step, and the ridge itself might be compared to the ingenious contrivance which surmounts the walls of gaols with a nicely balanced pile of loose bricks—supposing the interstices in this case to be filled with snow. We crept, however, cautiously along the parapet, glancing down the mighty cliffs beneath us, and then, at two steps more, we proudly stepped (at 11.40) on to the little level platform which forms the "allerhöchste Spitze" of the Schreckhorn.

I need hardly remark that our first proceeding was to give a hearty cheer, which was faintly returned by the friends who were still watching us from the Strahleck. My next was to sit down, in the warm and perfectly calm summer air, to enjoy a pipe and the beauties of nature, whilst my guides erected a cairn of stones round a large black flag which we had brought up to confute cavillers. Mountain tops are always more or less impressive in one way—namely, from the giddy cliffs which surround them. But the more distant prospects from them may be divided into two classes: those from the Wetterhorn, Jungfrau, or Monte Rosa, and other similar mountains, which include on one side the lowland countries, forming a contrast to the rough mountain ranges; and those from mountains standing, not on the edge, but in the very centre of the regions of frost and desolation. The Schreckhorn (like the Finsteraarhorn) is a grand example of this latter kind. Four great glaciers seem to radiate from its base. The great Oberland peaks— the Finsteraarhorn, Jungfrau, Mönch, Eiger, and Wetterhorn—stand round in a grim circle, showing their bare faces of precipitous rock across the dreary wastes of snow. At your feet are the "urns of the silent snow," from which the glaciers of Grindelwald draw the supplies that enable them to descend far into the regions of cultivated land, trickling down like great damp icicles, of insignificant mass compared with these mighty reservoirs. You are in the centre of a whole district of desolation, suggesting a landscape from Greenland, or an imaginary picture of England in the glacial epoch, with shores yet unvisited by the irrepressible Gulf Stream. The charm of such views— little as they are generally appreciated by professed admirers of the picturesque—is to my taste unique, though not easily explained to unbelievers. They have a certain soothing influence, like slow and stately music, or one of the strange opium dreams described by De Quincey. If his journey in the mail-coach could have led him through an Alpine pass instead of the quiet Cumberland hills, he would have seen visions still more poetical than that of the minster in the "dream fugue." Unable as I am to bend his bow, I can only say that there is something almost unearthly in the sight of enormous spaces of hill and plain, apparently unsubstantial as a mountain mist, glimmering away to the indistinct horizon, and as it were spell-bound by an absolute and eternal silence. The sentiment may be very different when a storm is raging and nothing is visible but the black ribs of the mountains glaring at you through rents in the clouds; but on that perfect day on the top of the Schreckhorn, where not a wreath of vapour was to be seen under the whole vast canopy of the sky, a delicious lazy sense of calm repose was the appropriate frame of mind. One felt as if some immortal being, with no particular duties upon his hands, might be calmly sitting upon those desolate rocks and watching the little shadowy wrinkles of the plain, that were really mountain ranges, rise and fall through slow geological epochs. I had no companion to disturb my reverie or introduce discordant associations. An hour passed like a few minutes, but there were still difficulties to be encountered which would have made any longer delay unadvisable. I therefore added a few touches to our cairn, and then turned to the descent.

It is a general opinion, with which I do not agree, that the descent of slippery or difficult rock is harder than the ascent. My guides, however, seemed to be fully convinced of it; or perhaps they merely wished to prove, in opposition to my sceptical remarks, that there was some use in having three guides. Accordingly, whilst Christian Michel led the way, old Peter and Kaufmann persisted in planting themselves steadily in some safe nook, and then hauling at the rope round my waist. By a violent exertion and throwing all my weight on to the rope, I gradually got myself paid slowly out, and descended to the next ledge, feeling as if I should be impressed with a permanent groove to which ropes might be fixed in future. The process was laborious, not to say painful, and I was sincerely glad when the idea dawned upon the good fellows that I might be trusted to use my limbs more freely. *Surtout point de zèle* is occasionally a good motto for guides as well as ministers.

I have suffered worse things on awkward places from the irregular enthusiasm of my companions.

Never shall I forget a venerable guide at Kippel, whose glory depended on the fact that his name was mentioned in The Book, viz. *Murray's Guide*. Having done nothing all day to maintain his reputation, he seized a favourable opportunity as we were descending a narrow arête of snow, and suddenly clutching my coat-tails, on pretence of steadying me, brought me with a jerk into a sitting position. My urgent remonstrances only produced bursts of *patois,* mixed with complacent chucklings, and I was forced to resign myself to the fate of being pulled backwards, all in a heap, about every third step along the arête. The process gave the old gentleman such evident pleasure that I ceased to complain.

On the present occasion my guides were far more reasonable, and I would never complain of a little extra caution. We were soon going along steadily enough, though the slippery nature of the rocks, and the precautions necessary to avoid dislodging loose stones, made our progress rather slow. At length, however, with that instinct which good guides always show, and in which amateurs are most deficient, we came exactly to the point where we had left our knapsacks. We were now standing close to the ravine I have mentioned. Suddenly I heard a low hiss close by me, and looking round saw a stream of snow shooting rapidly down the gully, like a long white serpent. It was the most insidious enemy of the mountaineer—an avalanche; not such as thunders down the cliffs of the Jungfrau, ready to break every bone in your body, but the calm malicious avalanche which would take you quietly off your legs, wrap you up in a sheet of snow, and bury you in a crevasse for a few hundred years, without making any noise about it. The stream was so narrow and well defined that I could easily have stepped across it; still it was rather annoying, inasmuch as immediately below us was a broad fringe of snow ending in a bergschrund, the whole being in what travellers used to represent as the normal condition of mountain snow—such that a stone, or even a hasty expression, rashly dropped, would probably start an avalanche. Christian Michel showed himself equal to the occasion. Choosing a deep trench in the snow—the channel of one of these avalanches—from which the upper layer of snow was cut away, he turned his face to the slope and dug his toes deeply into the firmer snow beneath. We followed, trying in every way to secure our hold of the treacherous footing. Every little bit of snow that we kicked aside started a young avalanche on its own account. By degrees, however, we reached the edge of a very broad and repulsive-looking bergschrund. Unfixing the rope we gave Kaufmann one end, and sent him carefully across a long and very shaky-looking bridge of snow. He got safely across, and we cautiously followed him, one by one. As the last man reached the other side, we felt that our dangers were over. It was now about five o'clock.

We agreed to descend by the Strahleck. Great delay was caused by our discovering that even on the nearly level surface there was a sheet of ice formed, which required many a weary step to be cut. It was long before we could reach the rocks and take off the rope for a race home down the slopes of snow.

As we reached our burrow we were gratified with one of the most glorious sights of the mountains. A huge cloud, which looked at least as lofty as the Eiger, rested with one extremity of its base on the Eiger, and the other on the Mettenberg, shooting its white pinnacles high up into the sunshine above. Through the mighty arched gateway thus formed, we could see far over the successive ranges of inferior mountains, standing like flat shades one behind another. The lower slopes of the Mettenberg glowed with a deep blood-red, and the more distant hills passed through every shade of blue, purple, and rose-coloured hues, into the faint blue of the distant Jura, with one gleam of green sky beyond. In the midst of the hills the Lake of Thun lay, shining like gold. A few peals of thunder echoed along the glacier valley, telling us of the storm that was raging over Grindelwald.

It was half-past seven when we reached our lair. We consequently had to pass another night there—a necessity which would have been easily avoided by a little more activity in the morning.

It is a laudable custom to conclude narratives of mountain ascents by a compliment to the guides who have displayed their skill and courage. Here, however, I shall venture to deviate from the ordinary practice by recording an anecdote, which may be instructive, and which well deserves to be remembered by visitors to Grindelwald. The guides of the Oberland have an occasional weakness, which Englishmen cannot condemn with a very clear conscience, for the consumption of strong drink; and it happened that the younger Michel was one day descending the well-known path which leads from the châlet above the so-called Eismeer to Grindelwald in an unduly convivial frame of mind. Just above the point where mules are generally left, the path runs close to the edge of an overhanging cliff, the rocks below having been scooped out by the glacier in old days, when the glacier was several hundred feet above its present level. The dangerous place is guarded by a wooden rail, which unluckily terminates before the cliff is quite passed. Michel, guiding himself as it may be supposed by the rail, very naturally stepped over the cliff when the guidance was prematurely withdrawn. I cannot state the vertical height through which he must have fallen on to a bed of hard uncompromising rock. I think, however, that I am within the mark in saying that it cannot have been much less than a hundred feet. It would have been a less dangerous experiment to step from the roof of the tallest house in London to the kerbstone below. Michel lay at the bottom all night, and next morning shook himself, got up, and walked home sober, and with no broken bones. I submit two morals for the choice of my readers, being quite unable, after much reflection, to decide which is the more appropriate. The first is, Don't get drunk when you have to walk along the edge of an Alpine cliff; the second is, Get drunk if you are likely to fall over an Alpine cliff. In any case, see that Michel is in his normal state of sobriety when you take him for a guide, and carry the brandy-flask in your own pocket.

The First Ascent
of the Matterhorn

EDWARD WHYMPER

We started from Zermatt on the 13th of July 1865, at half-past five, on a brilliant and perfectly cloudless morning. We were eight in number—Croz, old Peter and his two sons, Lord F. Douglas, Hadow, Hudson, and I. To ensure steady motion, one tourist and one native walked together. The youngest Taugwalder fell to my share, and the lad marched well, proud to be on the expedition, and happy to show his powers. The wine-bags also fell to my lot to carry, and through-out the day, after each drink, I replenished them secretly with water, so that at the next halt they were found fuller than before! This was considered a good omen, and little short of miraculous.

On the first day we did not intend to ascend to any great height, and we mounted, accordingly, very leisurely; picked up the things which were left in the chapel at the Schwarzsee at 8.20, and proceeded thence along the ridge connecting the Hörnli with the Matterhorn. At half-past 11 we arrived at the base of the actual peak; then quitted the ridge, and clambered round some ledges on to the eastern face. We were now fairly upon the mountain, and were astonished to find that places which from the Riffel, or even from the Furggengletscher, looked entirely impracticable, were so easy that we could *run about*.

Before twelve o'clock we had found a good position for the tent, at a height of 11,000 feet. Croz and young Peter went on to see what was above, in order to save time on the following morning. They cut across the heads of the snow-slopes which descended towards the Furggengletscher, and disappeared round a corner; but shortly afterwards we saw them high up on the face, moving quickly. We others made a solid platform for the tent in a well-protected spot, and then watched eagerly for the return of the men. The stones which they upset told us that they were very high, and we supposed that the way must be easy. At length, just before 3 p.m., we saw them coming down, evidently much excited. "What are they saying, Peter?" "Gentlemen, they say it is no good." But when they came near we heard a different story. "Nothing but what was good; not a difficulty, not a single difficulty! We could have gone to the summit and returned to-day easily!"

We passed the remaining hours of daylight—some basking in the sunshine, some sketching or collecting; and when the sun went down, giving, as it departed, a glorious promise for the morrow, we returned to the tent to arrange for the night. Hudson made tea, I coffee, and we then retired each one to his blanket-bag—the Taugwalders, Lord Francis Douglas, and myself occupying the tent; the others remaining, by preference, outside. Long after dusk the cliffs above echoed with our laughter and with the songs of the guides; for we were happy that night in camp, and feared no evil.

We assembled together outside the tent before dawn on the morning of the 14th, and started directly it was light enough to move. Young Peter came on with us as a guide, and his brother returned to Zermatt. We followed the route which had been taken on the previous day, and in a few minutes turned the rib which had intercepted the view of the eastern face from our tent platform. The whole of this great slope was now revealed, rising for 3,000 feet like a huge natural staircase. Some parts were more and others were less easy; but we were not once brought to a halt by any serious impediment, for when an obstruction was met in front it could always be turned to the right or to the left. For the greater part of the way there was, indeed, no occasion for the rope, and sometimes Hudson led, sometimes myself. At 6.20 we had attained a height of

12,800 feet, and halted for half an hour; we then continued the ascent without a break until 9.55, when we stopped for fifty minutes, at a height of 14,000 feet. Twice we struck the NE ridge and followed it for some little distance—to no advantage, for it was usually more rotten and steep, and always more difficult than the face. Still, we kept near to it, lest stones perchance might fall.

We had now arrived at the foot of that part which, from the Riffelberg or from Zermatt, seems perpendicular or overhanging, and could no longer continue upon the eastern side. For a little distance we ascended by snow upon the arête—that is, the ridge—descending towards Zermatt, and then, by common consent, turned over to the right, or to the northern side. Before doing so, we made a change in the order of ascent. Croz went first, I followed, Hudson came third; Hadow and old Peter were last. "Now," said Croz, as he led off—"now for something altogether different." The work became difficult, and required caution. In some places there was little to hold, and it was desirable that those should be in front who were least likely to slip. The general slope of the mountain at this part was *less* than 40°, and snow had accumulated in, and had filled up, the interstices of the rock face, leaving only occasional fragments projecting here and there. These were at times covered with a thin film of ice, produced from the melting and refreezing of the snow. It was the counterpart, on a small scale, of the upper 700 feet of the Pointe des Ecrins; only there was this material difference—the face of the Ecrins was about, or exceeded, an angle of 50°, and the Matterhorn face was less than 40°. It was a place over which any fair mountaineer might pass in safety, and Mr. Hudson ascended this part, and, as far as I know, the entire mountain, without having the slightest assistance rendered to him upon any occasion. Sometimes, after I had taken a hand from Croz, or received a pull, I turned to offer the same to Hudson; but he invariably declined, saying it was not necessary. Mr. Hadow, however, was not accustomed to this kind of work, and required continual assistance. It is only fair to say that the difficulty which he found at this part arose simply and entirely from want of experience.

The solitary difficult part was of no great extent. We bore away over it at first, nearly horizontally, for a distance of about 400 feet; then ascended directly towards the summit for about 60 feet; and then doubled back to the ridge which descends towards Zermatt. A long stride round a rather awkward corner brought us to snow once more. The last doubt vanished! The Matterhorn was ours! Nothing but 200 feet of easy snow remained to be surmounted!

You must now carry your thoughts back to the seven Italians who started from Breuil on the 11th of July. Four days had passed since their departure, and we were tormented with anxiety lest they should arrive on the top before us. All the way up we had talked of them, and many false alarms of "men on the summit" had been raised. The higher we rose, the more intense became the excitement. What if we should be beaten at the last moment? The slope eased off, at length we could be detached, and Croz and I, dashing away, ran a neck-and-neck race, which ended in a dead heat. At 1.40 p.m. the world was at our feet, and the Matterhorn was conquered. Hurrah! Not a footstep could be seen.

It was not yet certain that we had not been beaten. The summit of the Matterhorn was formed of a rudely level ridge, about 350 feet long, and the Italians might have been at its farther extremity. I hastened to the southern end, scanning the snow right and left eagerly. Hurrah again—it was untrodden! "Where were the men?" I peered over the cliff, half doubting, half expectant, and saw them immediately—mere dots on the ridge, at an immense distance below. Up went my arms and my hat. "Croz! Croz! come here!" "Where are they, Monsieur?" "There—don't you see them—down there!" "Ah! the *coquins*, they are low down." "Croz, we must make those fellows hear us." We yelled until we were hoarse. The Italians seemed to regard us—we could not be certain. "Croz, we *must* make them hear us; they *shall* hear us!" I seized a block of rock and hurled it down, and called upon my companion, in the name of friendship, to do the same. We drove our sticks in, and prized away the crags, and soon a torrent of stones poured down the cliffs. There was no mistake about it this time. The Italians turned and fled.

Still, I would that the leader of that party could have stood with us at that moment, for our victorious shouts conveyed to him the disappointment of the ambition of a lifetime. He was *the* man, of all those who attempted the ascent of the Matterhorn, who most deserved to be the first upon its summit. He was the first to doubt its inaccessibility, and he was the only man who persisted in believing that its ascent would be accomplished. It was the aim of his life to make the ascent from the side of Italy, for the honour of his native valley. For a time he had the game in his hands: he played it as he thought best; but he made a false move, and he lost it.

The others had arrived, so we went back to the northern end of the ridge. Croz now took the tent-pole, and planted it in the highest snow. "Yes," we said, "there is the flagstaff, but where is the flag?" "Here it is," he answered, pulling off his blouse and fixing it to the stick. It made a poor flag, and there was no wind to float it out, yet it was seen all around. They saw it at Zermatt—at the Riffel—in the Val Tournanche. At Breuil the watchers cried, "Victory is ours!" They raised "bravos" for Carrel and "vivas" for Italy, and hastened to put themselves *en fête*. On the morrow they were undeceived. "All was changed;

the explorers returned sad—cast down—disheartened—confounded—gloomy." "It is true," said the men. "We saw them ourselves—they hurled stones at us! The old traditions *are* true—there are spirits on the top of the Matterhorn!"

We returned to the southern end of the ridge to build a cairn, and then paid homage to the view. The day was one of those superlatively calm and clear ones which usually precede bad weather. The atmosphere was perfectly still, and free from all clouds or vapours. Mountains fifty—nay a hundred—miles off, looked sharp and near. All their details—ridge and crag, snow and glacier—stood out with faultless definition. Pleasant thoughts of happy days in bygone years came up unbidden, as we recognized the old familiar forms. All were revealed—not one of the principal peaks of the Alps was hidden. I see them clearly now—the great inner circles of giants, backed by the ranges, chains, and *massifs*. First came the Dent Blanche, hoary and grand; the Gabelhorn and pointed Rothhorn; and then the peerless Weisshorn: the towering Mischabelhörner, flanked by the Allaleinhorn, Strahlhorn, and Rimpfischhorn; then Monte Rosa—with its many Spitzes—the Lyskamm and the Breithorn. Behind were the Bernese Oberland, governed by the Finsteraarhorn; the Simplon and St. Gothard groups; the Disgrazia and the Orteler. Towards the south we looked down to Chivasso, on the plain of Piedmont, and far beyond. The Viso—

one hundred miles away—seemed close upon us; the Maritime Alps—one hundred and thirty miles distant—were free from haze. Then came my first love—the Pelvoux; the Ecrins and the Meije; the clusters of the Graians; and lastly, in the west, glowing in full sunlight, rose the monarch of all—Mont Blanc. Ten thousand feet beneath us were the green fields of Zermatt, dotted with châlets, from which blue smoke rose lazily. Eight thousand feet below, on the other side, were the pastures of Breuil. There were forests black and gloomy, and meadows bright and lively; bounding waterfalls and tranquil lakes; fertile lands and savage wastes; sunny plains and frigid *plateaux*. There were the most rugged forms, and the most graceful outlines—bold, perpendicular cliffs, and gentle, undulating slopes; rocky mountains and snowy mountains, sombre and solemn, or glittering and white, with walls—turrets—pinnacles—pyramids—domes—cones—and spires! There was every combination that the world can give, and every contrast that the heart could desire.

We remained on the summit for one hour—

"One crowded hour of glorious life."

It passed away too quickly, and we began to prepare for the descent.

The Descent
of the Matterhorn

EDWARD WHYMPER

Hudson and I again consulted as to the best and safest arrangement of the party. We agreed that it would be best for Croz to go first, and Hadow second; Hudson, who was almost equal to a born mountaineer in sureness of foot, wished to be third; Lord Francis Douglas was placed next; and old Peter, the strongest of the remainder, after him. I suggested to Hudson that we should attach a rope to the rocks on our arrival at the difficult bit, and hold it as we descended, as an additional protection. He approved the idea, but it was not definitely settled that it should be done. The party was being arranged in the above order whilst I was sketching the summit, and they had finished, and were waiting for me to be tied in line, when some one remembered that our names had not been left in a bottle. They requested me to write them down, and moved off while it was being done.

A few minutes afterwards I tied myself to young Peter, ran down after the others, and caught them just as they were commencing the descent of the difficult part. Great care was being taken. Only one man was moving at a time; when he was firmly planted the next advanced, and so on. They had not, however, attached the additional rope to rocks, and nothing was said about it. The suggestion was not made for my own sake, and I am not sure that it even occurred to me again. For some little distance we two followed the others, detached from them, and should have continued so had not Lord Francis Douglas asked me, about 3 p.m., to tie on to old Peter, as he feared, he said, that Taugwalder would not be able to hold his ground if a slip occurred.

A few minutes later a sharp-eyed lad ran into the Monte Rosa hotel, to Seiler, saying that he had seen an avalanche fall from the summit of the Matterhorn on to the Matterhorngletscher. The boy was reproved for telling idle stories; he was right, nevertheless, and this was what he saw.

Michel Croz had laid aside his axe, and in order to give Mr. Hadow greater security, was absolutely taking hold of his legs, and putting his feet, one by one, into their proper positions. So far as I know, no one was actually descending. I cannot speak with certainty, because the two leading men were partially hidden from my sight by an intervening mass of rock, but it is my belief, from the movements of their shoulders, that Croz, having done as I have said, was in the act of turning round, to go down a step or two himself; at this moment Mr. Hadow slipped, fell against him, and knocked him over. I heard one startled exclamation from Croz, then saw him and Mr. Hadow flying downwards; in another moment Hudson was dragged from his steps, and Lord F. Douglas immediately after him. All this was the work of a moment. Immediately we heard Croz's exclamation, old Peter and I planted ourselves as firmly as the rocks would permit: the rope was taut between us, and the jerk came on us both as on one man. We held; but the rope broke midway between Taugwalder and Lord Francis Douglas. For a few seconds we saw our unfortunate companions sliding downwards on their backs, and spreading out their hands, endeavouring to save themselves. They passed from our sight uninjured, disappeared one by one, and fell from precipice to precipice on to the Matterhorngletscher below, a distance of nearly 4,000 feet in height. From the moment the rope broke it was impossible to help them.

So perished our comrades! For the space of half an hour we remained on the spot without moving a single step. The two men, paralyzed by terror, cried like infants, and trembled in such a manner as to threaten us with the fate of the others. Old Peter rent the air with exclamations of "Chamounix! Oh, what will Chamounix say?" He meant, Who would believe that Croz could fall? The young man did nothing but scream or sob, "We are lost! we are lost!" Fixed between the two, I could neither move up nor down. I begged young Peter to descend, but he dared not. Unless he did we could not advance. Old Peter became alive to the danger, and swelled the cry, "We are lost! we are lost!" The father's fear was natural—he trembled for his son; the young man's fear was cowardly—he thought of self alone. At last old Peter summoned up courage, and changed his position to a rock to which he could fix the rope; the young man then descended, and we all stood together. Immediately we did so I asked for the rope which had given way, and found, to my surprise—indeed to my horror—that it was the weakest of the three ropes. It was not brought, and should not have been employed, for the purpose for which it was used. It was old rope, and, compared with the others, was feeble. It was intended as a reserve, in case we had to leave much rope behind, attached to rocks. I saw at once that a serious question was involved, and made him give me the end. It had broken in mid-air, and it did not appear to have sustained previous injury.

For more than two hours afterwards I thought almost every moment that the next would be my last; for the Taugwalders, utterly unnerved, were not only incapable of giving assistance, but were in such a state that a slip might have been expected from them at any moment. After a time we were able to do that which should have been done at first, and fixed rope to firm rocks, in addition to being tied together. These ropes were cut from time to time, and were left behind. Even with their assurance the men were afraid to proceed, and several times old Peter turned with ashy face and faltering limbs, and said, with terrible emphasis, "*I cannot!*"

About 6 p.m. we arrived at the snow upon the ridge descending towards Zermatt, and all peril was over. We frequently looked, but in vain, for traces of our unfortunate companions; we bent over the ridge and cried to them, but no sound returned. Convinced at last that they were neither within sight nor hearing, we ceased from our useless efforts, and, too cast down for speech, silently gathered up our things, and the little effects of those who were lost, preparatory to continuing the descent; when, lo! a mighty arch appeared, rising above the Lyskamm, high into the sky. Pale, colourless, and noiseless, but perfectly sharp and defined, except where it was lost in the clouds, this unearthly apparition seemed like a vision from another world; and, almost appalled, we watched with amazement the gradual development of two vast crosses, one on either side. If the Taugwalders had not been the first to perceive it, I should have doubted my senses. They thought it had some connection with the accident, and I, after a while, that it might bear some relation to ourselves. But our movements had no effect upon it. The spectral forms remained motionless. It was a fearful and wonderful sight; unique in my experience, and impressive beyond description, coming at such a moment.

I was ready to leave, and waiting for the others. They had recovered their appetites and the use of their tongues. They spoke in patois, which I did not understand. At length the son said in French, "Monsieur." "Yes." "We are poor men; we have lost our Herr; we shall not get paid; we can ill afford this." "Stop!" I said, interrupting him, "that is nonsense. I shall pay you, of course, just as if your Herr were here." They talked together in their patois for a short time, and then the son spoke again. "We don't wish you to pay us. We wish you to write in the hotel-book at Zermatt, and to your journals, that we have not been paid." "What nonsense are you talking? I don't understand you. What do you mean?" He proceeded, "Why, next year there will be many travellers at Zermatt, and we shall get more *voyageurs*."

Who would answer such a proposition? I made them no reply in words, but they knew very well the indignation that I felt. They filled the cup of bitterness to overflowing, and I tore down the cliff, madly and recklessly, in a way that caused them, more than once, to inquire if I wished to kill them.

Night fell, and for an hour the descent was continued in the darkness. At half-past 9 a resting-place was found, and upon a wretched slab, barely large enough to hold the three, we passed six miserable hours. At daybreak the descent was resumed, and from the Hörnli ridge we ran down to the châlets of Buhl, and on to Zermatt. Seiler met me at his door, and followed in silence to my room. "What is the matter?" "The Taugwalders and I have returned." He did not need more, and burst into tears; but lost no time in useless lamentations, and set to work to arouse the village. Ere long a score of men had started to ascend the Hohlicht heights, above Kalbermatt and Z'Mutt, which commanded the plateau of the Matterhorngletscher. They returned after six hours, and reported that they had seen the bodies lying motionless on the snow. This was on Saturday; and they proposed that we should leave on Sunday evening, so as to arrive upon the plateau at daybreak on Monday. Unwilling to lose the slightest chance, the Rev. J. M'Cormick and I resolved to start on Sunday morning. The Zermatt men, threatened with excommunication by their priests if they failed to attend the early mass, were unable to accompany us. To several of them, at least, this was a severe trial. Peter Perrn declared with tears that nothing else would have prevented him from joining in the search for his old comrades. Englishmen came to our aid. The Rev. J. Robertson and Mr. J.

Phillpotts offered themselves, and their guide Franz Andermatten; another Englishman lent us Joseph Marie and Alexandre Lochmatter. Frédéric Payot, and Jean Tairraz of Chamounix, also volunteered.

We started at 2 a.m. on Sunday the 16th, and followed the route that we had taken on the previous Thursday as far as the Hörnli. Thence we went down to the right of the ridge, and mounted through the *séracs* of the Matterhorngletscher. By 8.30 we had got to the plateau at the top of the glacier, and within sight of the corner in which we knew my companions must be. As we saw one weather-beaten man after another raise the telescope, turn deadly pale, and pass it on without a word to the next, we knew that all hope was gone. We approached. They had fallen below as they had fallen above—Croz a little in advance, Hadow near him, and Hudson some distance behind; but of Lord Francis Douglas we could see nothing. We left them where they fell, buried in snow at the base of the grandest cliff of the most majestic mountain of the Alps.

All those who had fallen had been tied with the Manilla, or with the second and equally strong rope, and consequently there had been only one link— that between old Peter and Lord Francis Douglas— where the weaker rope had been used. This had a very ugly look for Taugwalder, for it was not possible to suppose that the others would have sanctioned the employment of a rope so greatly inferior in strength when there were more than two hundred and fifty feet of the better qualities still remaining out of use. For the sake of the old guide (who bore a good reputation), and upon all other accounts, it was desirable that this matter should be cleared up; and after my examination before the court of inquiry which was instituted by the Government was over, I handed in a number of questions which were framed so as to afford old Peter an opportunity of exculpating himself from the grave suspicions which at once fell upon him. The questions, I was told, were put and answered; but the answers, although promised, have never reached me.

Meanwhile, the administration sent strict injunctions to recover the bodies, and upon the 19th of July twenty-one men of Zermatt accomplished that sad and dangerous task. Of the body of Lord Francis Douglas they, too, saw nothing; it was probably still arrested on the rocks above. The remains of Hudson and Hadow were interred upon the north side of the Zermatt Church, in the presence of a reverent crowd of sympathizing friends. The body of Michel Croz lies upon the other side, under a simpler tomb, whose inscription bears honourable testimony to his rectitude, to his courage, and to his devotion.

So the traditional inaccessibility of the Matterhorn was vanquished, and was replaced by legends of a more real character. Others will essay to scale its proud cliffs, but to none will it be the mountain that it was to its early explorers. Others may tread its summit-snows, but none will ever know the feelings of those who first gazed upon its marvellous panorama; and none, I trust, will ever be compelled to tell of joy turned into grief, and of laughter into mourning. It proved to be a stubborn foe; it resisted long, and gave many a hard blow; it was defeated at last with an ease that none could have anticipated, but, like a relentless enemy—conquered but not crushed—it took terrible vengeance. The time may come when the Matterhorn shall have passed away, and nothing, save a heap of shapeless fragments, will mark the spot where the great mountain stood; for, atom by atom, inch by inch, and yard by yard, it yields to forces which nothing can withstand. That time is far distant; and ages hence generations unborn will gaze upon its awful precipices and wonder at its unique form. However exalted may be their ideas, and however exaggerated their expectations, none will come to return disappointed!

The play is over, and the curtain is about to fall. Before we part, a word upon the graver teachings of the mountains. See yonder height! 'Tis far away; unbidden comes the word "Impossible!" "Not so," says the mountaineer. "The way is long, I know; it's difficult—it may be—dangerous. It's possible, I'm sure; I'll seek the way; take counsel of my brother mountaineers, and find how they have gained similar heights, and learned to avoid the dangers." He starts (all slumbering down below); the path is slippery—may be laborious too. Caution and perseverance gain the day—the height is reached! and those beneath cry, "Incredible; 'tis superhuman!"

We who go mountain-scrambling have constantly set before us the superiority of fixed purpose or perseverance to brute force. We know that each height, each step, must be gained by patient, laborious toil, and that wishing cannot take the place of working; we know the benefits of mutual aid; that many a difficulty must be encountered, and many an obstacle must be grappled with or turned; but we know that where there's a will there's a way: and we come back to our daily occupations better fitted to fight the battle of life, and to overcome the impediments which obstruct our paths, strengthened and cheered by the recollection of past labours, and by the memories of victories gained in other fields.

I have not made myself either an advocate or an apologist for mountaineering, nor do I now intend to usurp the functions of a moralist; but my task would have been ill performed if it had been concluded without one reference to the more serious lessons of the mountaineer. We glory in the physical regeneration which is the product of our exertions; we exult over the grandeur of the scenes that are brought before our eyes, the splendours of sunrise and sunset, and the beauties of hill, dale, lake, wood, and water-fall; but we value more highly the development of manliness, and the evolution, under combat with difficulties, of those noble qualities of human nature—courage, patience, endurance, and fortitude.

Some hold these virtues in less estimation, and assign base and contemptible motives to those who indulge in our innocent sport.

"Be thou chaste as ice, as pure as snow, thou shalt not escape calumny."

Others, again, who are not detractors, find mountaineering, as a sport, to be wholly unintelligible. It is not greatly to be wondered at—we are not all constituted alike. Mountaineering is a pursuit essentially adapted to the young or vigorous, and not to the old or feeble. To the latter, toil may be no pleasure; and it is often said by such persons, "This man is making a toil of pleasure." Toil he must who goes mountaineering; but out of the toil comes strength (not merely muscular energy—more than that), an awakening of all the faculties; and from the strength arises pleasure. Then, again, it is often asked, in tones which seem to imply that the answer must at least be doubtful, "But does it repay you?" Well, we cannot estimate our enjoyment as you measure your wine or weigh your lead; it is real, nevertheless. If I could blot out every reminiscence or erase every memory, still I should say that my scrambles amongst the Alps have repaid me, for they have given me two of the best things a man can possess— health and friends.

The recollections of past pleasures cannot be effaced. Even now as I write they crowd up before me. First comes an endless series of pictures, magnificent in form, effect, and colour. I see the great peaks, with clouded tops, seeming to mount up for ever and ever; I hear the music of the distant herds, the peasant's jodel, and the solemn church bells; and I scent the fragrant breath of the pines: and after these have passed away another train of thoughts succeeds—of those who have been upright, brave, and true; of kind hearts and bold deeds; and of courtesies received at stranger hands, trifles in themselves, but expressive of that good will towards men which is the essence of charity.

Still, the last, sad memory hovers round, and sometimes drifts across like floating mist, cutting off sunshine, and chilling the remembrance of happier times. There have been joys too great to be described in words, and there have been griefs upon which I have not dared to dwell; and with these in mind I say, Climb if you will, but remember that courage and strength are naught without prudence, and that a momentary negligence may destroy the happiness of a lifetime. Do nothing in haste; look well to each step; and from the beginning think what may be the end.

The Ascent of Mount Takhoma [Mount Rainier]

GENERAL HAZARD STEVENS

When Vancouver, in 1792, penetrated the Straits of Fuca and explored the unknown waters of the Mediterranean of the Pacific, wherever he sailed, from the Gulf of Georgia to the farthest inlet of Puget Sound, he beheld the lofty, snow-clad barrier range of the Cascades stretching north and south and bounding the eastern horizon. Towering at twice the altitude of all others, at intervals of a hundred miles there loomed up above the range three majestic, snowy peaks that

> "Like giants stand,
> To sentinel enchanted land."

In the matter-of-fact spirit of a British sailor of his time, he named these sublime monuments of nature in honor of three lords of the English admiralty, Hood, Rainier, and Baker. Of these Rainier is the central, situated about half-way between the Columbia River and the line of British Columbia, and is by far the loftiest and largest. Its altitude is 14,444 feet, while Hood is 11,025 feet, and Baker is 10,810 feet high. The others, too, are single cones, while Rainier, or Takhoma,[1] is an immense mountain-mass with three distinct peaks, an eastern, a northern, and a southern; the two last extending out and up from the main central dome, from the summit of which they stand over a mile distant, while they are nearly two miles apart from each other.

Takhoma overlooks Puget Sound from Olympia to Victoria, one hundred and sixty miles. Its snow-clad dome is visible from Portland on the Willamette, one hundred and twenty miles south, and from the table-land of Walla Walla, one hundred and fifty miles east. A region two hundred and fifty miles across, including nearly all of Washington Territory, part of Oregon, and part of Idaho, is commanded in one field of vision by this colossus among mountains.

Takhoma had never been ascended. It was a virgin peak. The superstitious fears and traditions of the Indians, as well as the dangers of the ascent, had prevented their attempting to reach the summit, and the failure of a gallant and energetic officer, whose courage and hardihood were abundantly shown during the rebellion, had in general estimation proved it insurmountable.

For two years I had resolved to ascend Takhoma, but both seasons the dense smoke overspreading the whole country had prevented the attempt. Mr. Philomon Beecher Van Trump, humorous, generous, whole-souled, with endurance and experience withal, for he had roughed it in the mines, and a poetic appreciation of the picturesque and the sublime, was equally eager to scale the summit. Mr. Edward T. Coleman, an English gentleman of Victoria, a landscape artist and an Alpine tourist, whose reputed experience in Switzerland had raised a high opinion of his ability above the snow-line, completed the party.

Olympia, the capital of Washington Territory, is a beautiful, maple-embowered town of some two thousand inhabitants, situated at the southernmost extremity of Puget Sound, and west of Takhoma, distant in an air line seventy-five miles. The intervening country is covered with dense fir forests, almost impenetrable to the midday sun, and obstructed with fallen trees, upturned roots and stumps, and a perfect jungle of undergrowth, through which the most energetic traveler can accomplish but eight or nine miles a day. It was advisable to gain the nearest possible point by some trail, before plunging into the unbroken forest. The Nisqually River, which rises on the southern and western slopes of Takhoma, and empties into the sound a few miles north of Olympia, offered the most direct and natural approach. Ten years before, moreover, a few enterprising settlers had blazed out a trail across the Cascade Range, which followed the Nisqually nearly up to its source, thence deflected south to the Cowlitz River, and pursued this stream in a northeastern course to the summit of the range, thus turning the great mountain by a wide circuit. The best-informed mountain men represented the approaches on the south and southeast as by far the most favorable. The Nisqually-Cowlitz trail, then, seemed much the best, for the Nisqually, heading in the south and southwest slopes, and the Cowlitz, in the southeastern, afforded two lines of approach, by either of which the distance to the mountain, after leaving the trail, could not exceed thirty miles.

One August afternoon, Van Trump and I drove out to Yelm Prairie, thirty miles east of Olympia, and on the Nisqually River. We dashed rapidly on over a smooth, hard, level road, traversing wide reaches of prairie, passing under open groves of oaks and firs, and plunging through masses of black, dense forest in ever-changing variety. The moon had risen as we emerged upon Yelm Prairie; Takhoma, bathed in cold, white, spectral light from summit to base, appeared startlingly near and distinct. Our admiration was not so noisy as usual. Perhaps a little of dread mingled with it. In another hour we drove nearly across the plain and turned into a lane which conducted us up a beautiful rising plateau, crowned with a noble grove of oaks and overlooking the whole prairie. A comfortable, roomy house with a wide porch nestled among the trees, and its hospitable owner, Mr. James Longmire, appeared at the door and bade us enter.

The next morning we applied to Mr. Longmire for a guide, and for his advice as to our proposed trip. He was one of the few who marked out the Nisqually-Cowlitz trail years ago. He had explored the mountains about Takhoma as thoroughly, perhaps, as any other white man. One of the earliest settlers, quiet, self-reliant, sensible, and kindly, a better counselor than he could not have been found. The trail, he said, had not been traveled for four years, and was entirely illegible to eyes not well versed in woodcraft, and it would be folly for any one to attempt to follow it who was not thoroughly acquainted with the country. He could not leave his harvest, and moreover in three weeks he was to cross the mountains for a drove of cattle. His wife, too, quietly discouraged his going. She described his appearance on his return from previous mountain trips, looking as haggard and thin as though he had just risen from a sick-bed. She threw out effective little sketches of toil, discomfort, and hardship incident to mountain travel, and dwelt upon the hard fare. The bountiful country breakfast heaped before us, the rich cream, fresh butter and eggs, snowy, melting biscuits, and broiled chicken, with rich, white gravy, heightened the effect of her words.

But at length, when it appeared that no one else who knew the trail could be found, Mr. Longmire yielded to our persuasions, and consented to conduct us as far as the trail led, and to procure an Indian guide before leaving us to our own resources. As soon as we returned home we went with Mr. Coleman to his room to see a few indispensable equipments he had provided, in order that we might procure similar ones. The floor was literally covered with his traps, and he exhibited them one by one, expatiating upon their various uses. There was his ground-sheet, a large gum blanket equally serviceable to Mr. Coleman as a tent in camp and a bathtub at the hotel. There was a strong rope to which we were all to be tied when climbing the snow-fields, so that if one fell into a chasm the others could hold him up. The "creepers" were a clumsy, heavy arrangement of iron spikes made to fasten on the foot with chains and straps, in order to prevent slipping on the ice. He had an ice-axe for cutting steps, a spirit-lamp for making tea on the mountains, green goggles for snow-blindness, deer's fat for the face, Alpine staffs, needles and thread, twine, tacks, screws, screwdriver, gimlet, file, several medical prescriptions, two boards for pressing flowers, sketching materials, and in fact every article that Mr. Coleman in his extensive reading had found used or recommended by travelers. Every one of these he regarded as indispensable. The Alpine staff was, he declared, most important of all, a great assistance in traveling through the woods as well as on the ice; and he illustrated on his hands and knees how to cross a crevasse in the ice on two staffs. This interview naturally brought to mind the characteristic incident related of Packwood, the mountain man who, as hunter and prospector, had explored the deepest recesses of the Cascades. He had been engaged to guide a railroad surveying party across the mountains, and just as the party was about to start he approached the chief and demanded an advance to enable him to buy his outfit for the trip. "How much do you want?" asked the chief, rather anxiously, lest Packwood should overdraw his prospective wages. "Well, about two dollars and a half," was the reply; and at the camp-fire that evening, being asked if he had bought his outfit, Packwood, thrusting his hand into his pocket, drew forth and exhibited with perfect seriousness and complacency his entire outfit,—a jack-knife and a plug of tobacco.

Half a dozen carriages rattled gayly out of Olympia in the cool of the morning, filled with a laughing, singing, frolicking bevy of young ladies and gentlemen. They were the Takhoma party starting on their adventurous trip, with a chosen escort accompanying them to their first camp. They rested several hours at Longmire's during the heat of the day, and the drive was then continued seven miles farther, to the Lacamas, an irregular-shaped prairie two miles in length by half a mile in breadth. Here live two of Mr. Longmire's sons. Their farms form the last settlement, and at the gate of Mr. Elkane Longmire's house the road ends. A wooded knoll overlooking the prairie, with a spring of water at its foot, was selected as the camp-ground. Some of the party stretched a large sail between the trees as a tent, others watered and fed the horses, and others busied themselves with the supper. Two eager sportsmen started after grouse, while their more practical companions bought half a dozen chickens, and had them soon dressed and sputtering over the fire. The shades of night were falling as the party sat down on the ground and partook of a repast fit for the Olympians, and with a relish sharpened by the long journey and a whole day's fast.

Early in the morning Mr. Longmire arrived in camp with two mules and a pack-horse, and our mountain outfit was rapidly made up into suitable bales and packed upon the horse and one of the mules, the other mule being reserved for Longmire's own riding. We assembled around the breakfast with spirits as gay and appetites as sharp as ever. Then, with many good-bys and much waving of handker- chiefs, the party broke up. Four roughly clad pedes- trians moved off in single file, leading their pack animals, and looking back at every step to catch the last glimpse of the bright garments and fluttering cambrics, while the carriages drove rapidly down the road and disappeared in the dark, sullen forest.

We stepped off briskly, following a dim trail in an easterly course, and crossing the little prairie entered the timber. After winding over hilly ground for about three miles, we descended into the Nisqually bottom and forded a fine brook at the foot of the hill. For the next ten miles our route lay across the bottom, and along the bank of the river, passing around logs, following old, dry beds of the river and its lateral sloughs, ankle-deep in loose sand, and forcing our way through dense jungles of vine-maple. The trail was scarcely visible, and much obstructed by fallen trees and underbrush, and its difficulties were aggravated by the bewildering tracks of Indians who had lately wandered about the bottom in search of berries or rushes. We repeatedly missed the trail, and lost hours in retracing our steps and searching for the right course. The weather was hot and sultry, and rendered more oppressive by the dense foliage; myriads of gnats and mosquitoes tormented us and drove our poor animals almost frantic; and our thirst, aggravated by the severe and unaccustomed toil, seemed quenchless. At length we reached the ford of the Nisqually. Directly opposite, a perpendicular bluff of sand and gravel in alternate strata rose to the height of two hundred and fifty feet, its base washed by the river and its top crowned with firs. The stream was a hundred yards wide, waist-deep, and very rapid. Its waters were icy cold, and of a milk-white hue. This color is the characteristic of glacial rivers. The impalpable powder of thousands of tons of solid rocks ground up beneath the vast weight and resistless though imperceptible flow of huge glaciers, remains in solution in these streams, and colors them milk-white to the sea. Leading the animals down the bank and over a wide, dry bar of cobblestones, we stood at the brink of the swift, turbulent river, and prepared to essay its passage. Coleman mounted behind Van Trump on the little saddle-mule, his long legs dangling nearly to the ground, one hand grasping his Alpine staff, the other the neck-rope of the pack-mule, which Longmire bestrode. Longmire led in turn the pack-horse, behind whose bulky load was perched the other member of the party. The cavalcade, linked together in this order, had but just entered the stream when Coleman dropped the neckrope he was holding. The mule, bewildered by the rush and roar of the waters, turned directly down-stream, and in another instant our two pack animals, with their riders, would have been swept away in the furious rapids, had not Longmire with great presence of mind turned their erratic course in the right direction and safely brought them to the opposite shore. Following the bottom along the river for some distance, we climbed up the end of the bluff already mentioned, by a steep zigzag trail, and skirted along its brink for a mile. Far below us on the right rushed the Nisqually. On the left the bluff fell off in a steep hill-side thickly clothed with woods and underbrush, and at its foot plowed the Owhap, a large stream emptying into the Nisqually just below our ford. Another mile through the woods brought us out upon the Mishell Prairie, a beautiful, oval meadow of a hundred acres, embowered in the tall, dense fir forest, with a grove of lofty, branching oaks at its farther extremity, and covered with green grass and bright flowers. It takes its name from the Mishell River, which empties into the Nisqually a mile above the prairie.

We had marched sixteen miles. The packs were gladly thrown off beneath a lofty fir; the animals were staked out to graze. A spring in the edge of the woods afforded water, and while Mr. Coleman busied himself with his pipe, his flask, his note-book, his sketch-book, and his pouch of multifarious odds and ends, the other members of the party performed the duties incident to camp-life: made the fire, brought water, spread the blankets, and prepared supper. The flags attached to our Alpine staffs waved gayly overhead, and the sight of their bright folds fluttering in the breeze deepened the fixed resolve to plant them on Takhoma's hoary head, and made failure seem impossible. Mr. Coleman announced the altitude of Mishell Prairie as eight hundred feet by barometer. By an unlucky fall the thermometer was broken.

The march was resumed early next morning. As we passed the lofty oaks at the end of the little prairie, "On that tree," said Longmire, pointing out one of the noblest, "Maxon's company hanged two Indians in the war of '56. Ski-hi and his band, after many depredations upon the settlements, were encamped on the Mishell, a mile distant, in fancied security, when Maxon and his men surprised them and cut off every soul except the two prisoners whom they hanged here."

For eight miles the trail led through thick woods, and then, after crossing a wide "burn," past a number of deserted Indian wigwams, where another trail from the Nisqually plains joined ours, it descended a gradual slope, traversed a swampy thicket and another mile of heavy timber, and debouched on the Mishell River. This is a fine, rapid, sparkling stream, knee-deep and forty feet wide, rippling and dashing over a gravelly bed with clear, cold, transparent water. The purity of the clear water, so unlike the yeasty Nisqually, proves that the Mishell is no glacial river. Rising in an outlying range to the northwest of Takhoma, it flows in a southwest course to its confluence with the Nisqually near our previous night's camp. We unsaddled for the noon-rest. Van Trump went up the stream, fishing; Longmire crossed to look out the trail ahead, and Coleman made tea solitaire.

An hour passed, and Longmire returned. "The trail is blind," said he, "and we have no time to lose." Just then Van Trump returned; and the little train was soon in readiness to resume the tramp. Longmire rode his mule across the stream, telling us to drive the pack-animals after him and follow by a convenient log near by. As the mule attempted to climb a low place in the opposite bank, which offered an apparently easy exit from the river, his hind legs sank in a quicksand, he sat down quickly, if not gracefully, and, not fancying that posture, threw himself clear under water. His dripping rider rose to his feet, flung the bridle-rein over his arm, and, springing up the bank at a more practicable point, strode along the trail with as little delay and as perfect unconcern as though an involuntary ducking was of no more moment than climbing over a log.

The trail was blind. Longmire scented it through thickets of salal, fern, and underbrush, stumbling over roots, vines, and hollows hidden in the rank vegetation, now climbing huge trunks that the animals could barely scramble over, and now laboriously working his way around some fallen giant and traveling two hundred yards in order to gain a dozen yards on the course. The packs, continually jammed against trees and shaken loose by this rough traveling, required frequent repacking—no small task. At the very top of a high, steep hill, up which we had laboriously zigzagged shortly after crossing the Mishell, the little packhorse, unable to sustain the weight of the pack, which had shifted all to one side, fell and rolled over and over to the bottom. Bringing up the goods and chattels one by one on our own shoulders to the top of the hill, we replaced the load and started again. The course was in a southerly direction, over high rolling ground of good clay soil, heavily timbered, with marshy swales at intervals, to the Nisqually River again, a distance of twelve miles. We encamped on a narrow flat between the high hill just descended and the wide and noisy river, near an old ruined log-hut, the former residence of a once famed Indian medicine man, who, after the laudable custom of his race, had expiated with his life his failure to cure a patient.

Early next morning we continued our laborious march along the right bank of the Nisqually. Towards noon we left the river, and after threading in an easterly course a perfect labyrinth of fallen timber for six miles, and forcing our way with much difficulty through the tangled jungle of an extensive vine-maple swamp, at length crossed Silver Creek and gladly threw off the packs for an hour's rest.

A short distance after crossing Silver Creek the trail emerged upon more open ground, and for the first time the Nisqually Valley lay spread out in view before us. On the left stretched a wall of steep, rocky mountains, standing parallel to the course of the river and extending far eastward, growing higher and steeper and more rugged as it receded from view. At the very extremity of this range Takhoma loomed aloft, its dome high above all others and its flanks extending far down into the valley, and all covered, dome and flanks, with snow of dazzling white, in striking contrast with the black basaltic mountains about it. Startlingly near it looked to our eyes, accustomed to the restricted views and gloom of the forest.

After our noon rest we continued our journey up the valley, twisting in and out among the numerous trunks of trees that encumbered the ground, and after several hours of tedious trudging struck our third camp on Copper Creek, the twin brother to Silver Creek, just at dusk. We were thoroughly tired, having made twenty miles in thirteen hours of hard traveling.

Starting at daylight next morning, we walked two miles over rough ground much broken by ravines, and then descended into the bed of the Nisqually at the mouth of Goat Creek, another fine stream which empties here. We continued our course along the river bed, stumbling over rocky bars and forcing our way through dense thickets of willow, for some distance, then ascended the steep bank, went around a high hill over four miles of execrable trail, and descended to the river again, only two miles above Goat Creek. At this point the Takhoma branch or North Fork joins the Nisqually. This stream rises on the west side of Takhoma, is nearly as large as the main river, and like it shows its glacial origin by its milk-white water and by its icy cold, terribly swift and furious torrent. Crossing the Takhoma branch, here thirty yards wide, we kept up the main river, crossing and recrossing the stream frequently, and toiling over rocky bars for four miles, a distance which consumed five hours, owing to the difficulties of the way. We then left the Nisqually, turning to the right and traveling in a southerly course, and followed up the bed of a swampy creek for half a mile, then crossed a level tract much obstructed with fallen timber, then ascended a burnt ridge, and followed it for two miles to a small, marshy prairie in a wide canyon or defile closed in by rugged mountains on either side, and camped beside a little rivulet on the east side of the prairie. This was Bear Prairie, the altitude of which by the barometer was 2630 feet. The canyon formed a low pass between the Nisqually and Cowlitz rivers, and the little rivulet near which we camped flowed into the latter stream. The whole region had been swept by fire: thousands of giant trunks stook blackened and lifeless, the picture of desolation.

As we were reclining on the ground around the campfire, enjoying the calm and beatific repose which comes to the toil-worn mountaineer after his hearty supper, one of these huge trunks, after several warning creaks, came toppling and falling directly over our camp. All rushed to one side or another to avoid the impending crash. As one member of the party, hastily catching up in one hand a frying-pan laden with tin plates and cups, and in the other the camp kettle half full of boiling water, was scrambling away, his foot tripped in a blackberry vine and he fell outstretched at full length, the much-prized utensils scattering far and wide, while the falling tree came thundering down in the rear, doing no other damage, however, than burying a pair of blankets.

The following day Longmire and the writer went down the canyon to its junction with the Cowlitz River, in search of a band of Indians who usually made their headquarters at this point, and among whom Longmire hoped to find some hunter familiar with the mountains who might guide us to the base of Takhoma. The tiny rivulet as we descended soon swelled to a large and furious torrent, and its bed filled nearly the whole bottom of the gorge. The mountains rose on both sides precipitously, and the traces of land-slides which had gouged vast furrows down their sides were frequent. With extreme toil and difficulty we made our way, continually wading the torrent, clambering over broken masses of rock which filled its bed, or clinging to the steep hillsides, and reached the Cowlitz at length after twelve miles of this fatiguing work, but only to find the Indian camp deserted. Further search, however, was re- warded by the discovery of a rude shelter formed of a few skins thrown over a framework of poles, beneath which sat a squaw at work upon a half- dressed deerskin. An infant and a naked child of per- haps four years lay on the ground near the fire in front. Beside the lodge and quietly watching our approach, of which he alone seemed aware, stood a tall, slender Indian clad in buckskin shirt and leg- gings, with a striped woolen breech-clout, and a singular head garniture which gave him a fierce and martial appearance. This consisted of an old military cap, the visor thickly studded with brassheaded nails, while a large circular brass article, which might have been the top of an oil-lamp, was fastened upon the crown. Several eagle feathers stuck in the crown and strips of fur sewed upon the sides completed the edifice, which, notwithstanding its components, appeared imposing rather than ridiculous. A long Hudson Bay gun, the stock also ornamented with brassheaded tacks, lay in the hollow of the Indian's shoulder.

He received us with great friendliness, yet not without dignity, shaking hands and motioning us to a seat beneath the rude shelter, while his squaw hastened to place before us suspicious-looking cakes of dried berries, apparently their only food. After a moderate indulgence in this delicacy, Longmire made known our wants. The Indian spoke fluently the Chinook jargon, that high-bred lingo invented by the old fur-traders. He called himself "Sluiskin," and readily agreed to guide us to Rainier, known to him only as Takhoma, and promised to report at Bear Prairie the next day. It was after seven in the evening when we reached camp, thoroughly fagged.

Punctual to promise, Sluiskin rode up at noon mounted upon a stunted Indian pony, while his squaw and pappooses followed upon another even more puny and forlorn. After devouring an enormous dinner, evidently compensating for the rigors of a long fast, in reply to our inquiries he described the route he proposed to take to Takhoma. Pointing to the almost perpendicular height immediately back or east of our camp, towering three thousand feet or more overhead, the loftiest mountain in sight, "We go to the top of that mountain to-day," said he, "and to-morrow we follow along the high, backbone ridge of the mountains, now up, now down, first on one side and then on the other, a long day's journey, and at last, descending far down from the mountains into a deep valley, reach the base of Takhoma." Sluiskin illustrated his Chinook with speaking signs and pantomine. He had frequently hunted the mountain sheep upon the snow-fields of Takhoma, but had never ascended to the summit. It was impossible to do so, and he put aside as idle talk our expressed intention of making the ascent.

We had already selected the indispensable articles for a week's tramp, a blanket apiece, the smallest coffee-pot and frying-pan, a scanty supply of bacon, flour, coffee, etc., and had made them up into suitable packs of forty pounds each, provided with slings like a knapsack, and had piled together under the lee of a huge fallen trunk our remaining goods. Longmire, who although impatient to return home, where his presence was urgently needed, had watched and directed our preparations during the forenoon with kindly solicitude, now bade us good-by: mounted on one mule and leading the other, he soon disappeared down the trail on his lonely, homeward way. He left us the little pack-horse, thinking it would be quite capable of carrying our diminished outfit after our return from Takhoma.

Sluiskin led the way. The load upon his shoulders was sustained by a broad band, passing over his head, upon which his heavy, brass-studded rifle, clasped in both hands, was poised and balanced. Leaving behind the last vestige of trail, we toiled in single file slowly and laboriously up the mountain all the afternoon. The steepness of the ascent in many places required the use of both hand and foot in climbing, and the exercise of great caution to keep the heavy packs from dragging us over backwards. Coleman lagged behind from the start, and at intervals his voice could be heard hallooing and calling upon us to wait. Towards sunset we reached a level terrace, or bench, near the summit, gladly threw off our packs, and waited for Coleman, who, we supposed, could not be far below. He not appearing, we hallooed again and again. No answer! We then sent Sluiskin down the mountain to his aid. After an hour's absence the Indian returned. He had descended, he said, a long distance, and at last caught sight of Coleman. He was near the foot of the mountain, had thrown away his pack, blankets and all, and was evidently returning to camp. And Sluiskin finished his account with expressions of contempt for the "cultus King George man." What was to be done?

Coleman carried in his pack all our bacon, our only supply of meat, except a few pounds of dried beef. He also had the barometer, the only instrument that had survived the jolts and tumbles of our rough trip. But, on the other hand, he had been a clog upon our march from the outset. He was evidently too infirm to endure the toil before us, and would not only be unable to reach, still less ascend Takhoma, but might even impede and frustrate our own efforts. Knowing that he would be safe in camp until our return, we hastily concluded to proceed without him, trusting to our rifles for a supply of meat.

Sluiskin led us along the side of the ridge in a southerly direction for two miles farther, to a well-sheltered, grassy hollow in the mountain-top, where he had often previously encamped. It was after dark when we reached this place. The usual spring had gone dry, and, parched with thirst we searched the gulches of the mountain-side for water an hour, but without success. At length the writer, recalling a scanty rill which trickled across their path a mile back, taking the coffee-pot and large canteen, retraced his steps, succeeded in filling these utensils after much fumbling in the dark and consequent delay, and returned to camp. He found Van Trump and the Indian, anxious at the long delay, mounted on the crest of the ridge some two hundred yards from camp, waving torches and shouting lustily to direct his steps. The mosquitoes and flies came in clouds, and were terribly annoying. After supper of coffee and bread, we drank up the water, rolled ourselves in our blankets, and lay down under a tree with our flags floating from under the boughs overhead. Hot as had been the day, the night was cold and frosty, owing, doubtless, to the altitude of our camp.

At the earliest dawn next morning we were moving on without breakfast, and parched with thirst. Sluiskin led us in a general course about north-northeast, but twisting to nearly every point of the compass, and climbing up and down thousands of feet from mountain to mountain, yet keeping on the highest backbone between the headwaters of the Nisqually and Cowlitz rivers. After several hours of this work we came to a well-sheltered hollow, one side filled with a broad bed of snow, at the foot of which nestled a tiny, tranquil lakelet, and gladly threw off our heavy packs, assuaged our thirst, and took breakfast—bread and coffee again. Early as it was, the chill of the frosty night still in the air, the mosquitoes renewed their attacks, and proved as innumerable and vexatious as ever.

Continuing our march, we crossed many beds of snow, and drank again and again from the icy rills which flowed out of them. The mountains were covered with stunted mountain-ash and low, stubby firs with short, bushy branches, and occasionally a few pines. Many slopes were destitute of trees but covered with luxuriant grass and the greatest profusion of beautiful flowers of vivid hues. This was especially the case with the southern slopes, while the northern sides of the mountains were generally wooded. We repeatedly ate berries, and an hour afterwards ascended to where berries of the same kind were found scarcely yet formed. The country was much obscured with smoke from heavy fires which had been raging on the Cowlitz the last two days. But when at length, after climbing for hours an almost perpendicular peak—creeping on hands and knees over loose rocks, and clinging to scanty tufts of grass where a single slip would have sent us rolling a thousand feet down to destruction—we reached the highest crest and looked over, we exclaimed that we were already well repaid for all our toil. Nothing can convey an idea of the grandeur and ruggedness of the mountains. Directly in front, and apparently not over two miles distant, although really twenty, old Takhoma loomed up more gigantic than ever. We were far above the level of the lower snow-line on Takhoma. The high peak upon which we clung seemed the central core or focus of all the mountains around, and on every side we looked down vertically thousands of feet, deep down into vast, terrible defiles, black and fir-clothed, which stretched away until lost in the distance and smoke. Between them, separating one from another, the mountain-walls rose precipitously and termi-nated in bare, columnar peaks of black basaltic or volcanic rock, as sharp as needles. It seemed incredible that any human foot could have followed out the course we came, as we looked back upon it.

After a few hours more of this climbing, we stood upon the summit of the last mountain-ridge that separated us from Takhoma. We were in a saddle of the ridge; a lofty peak rose on either side. Below us extended a long, steep hollow or gulch filled with snow, the farther extremity of which seemed to drop off perpendicularly into a deep valley or basin. Across this valley, directly in front, filling up the whole horizon and view with an indescribable aspect of magnitude and grandeur, stood the old leviathan of mountains. The broad, snowy dome rose far among and above the clouds. The sides fell off in vertical steeps and fearful black walls of rock for a third of its altitude; lower down, vast, broad, gently sloping snow-fields surrounded the mountain, and were broken here and there by ledges or masses of the dark basaltic rock protruding above them. Long, green ridges projected from this snow-belt at intervals, radiating from the mountain and extending many miles until lost in the distant forests. Deep valleys lay between these ridges. Each at its upper end formed the bed of a glacier, which closed and filled it up with solid ice. Below the snow-line bright green grass with countless flowers, whose vivid scarlet, blue, and purple formed bodies of color in the distance, clothed the whole region of ridges

and valleys, for a breadth of five miles. The beautiful
balsam firs, about thirty feet in height, and of a purple, dark-green color, stood scattered over the landscape, now singly, now in groves, and now in long
lines, as though planted in some well-kept park. Farther down an unbroken fir forest surrounded the
mountain and clad the lower portions of the ridges
and valleys. In every sheltered depression or hollow
lay beds of snow with tiny brooks and rivulets flowing from them. The glaciers terminated not gradually, but abruptly, with a wall of ice from one to five
hundred feet high, from beneath which yeasty torrents burst forth and rushed roaring and tumbling
down the valleys. The principal of these, far away on
our left front, could be seen plunging over two considerable falls, half hidden in the forest, while the
roar of waters was distinctly audible.

At length we cautiously descended the snow-bed,
and, climbing at least fifteen hundred feet down a
steep but ancient land-slide by means of the bushes
growing among the loose rocks, reached the valley,
and encountered a beautiful, peaceful, limpid creek.
Van Trump could not resist the temptation of
unpacking his bundle, selecting one of his carefully
preserved flies, and trying the stream for trout,
but without a single rise. After an hour's rest and
a hearty repast we resumed our packs, despite
Sluiskin's protests, who seemed tired out with his
arduous day's toil and pleaded hard against traveling

farther. Crossing the stream, we walked through several grassy glades, or meadows, alternating with open woods. We soon came to the foot of one of the long ridges already described, and ascending it followed it for several miles through open woods, until we emerged upon the enchanting emerald and flowery meads which clothe these upper regions. Halting upon a rising eminence in our course, and looking back, we beheld the ridge of mountains we had just descended stretching from east to west in a steep, rocky wall; a little to the left, a beautiful lake, evidently the source of the stream just crossed, which we called Clear Creek, and glimpses of which could be seen among the trees as it flowed away to the right, down a rapidly descending valley along the foot of the lofty mountain-wall. Beyond the lake again, still farther to the left, the land also subsided quickly. It was at once evident that the lake was upon a summit, or divide, between the waters of the Nisqually and Cowlitz rivers. The ridge which we were ascending lay north and south, and led directly up to the mountain.

We camped, as the twilight fell upon us, in an aromatic grove of balsam firs. A grouse, the fruit of Sluiskin's rifle, broiled before the fire, and impartially divided gave a relish to the dry bread and coffee. After supper we reclined upon our blankets in front of the bright, blazing fire, well satisfied. The Indian, when starting from Bear Prairie, had evidently deemed our intention of ascending Takhoma too absurd to deserve notice. The turning back of Mr. Coleman only deepened his contempt for our prowess. But his views had undergone a change with the day's march. The affair began to look serious to him, and now in Chinook, interspersed with a few words of broken English and many signs and gesticulations, he began a solemn exhortation and warning against our rash project.

Takhoma, he said, was an enchanted mountain, inhabited by an evil spirit, who dwelt in a fiery lake on its summit. No human being could ascend it or even attempt its ascent, and survive. At first, indeed, the way was easy. The broad snow-fields, over which he had so often hunted the mountain goat, interposed no obstacle, but above them the rash adventurer would be compelled to climb up steeps of loose, rolling rocks, which would turn beneath his feet and cast him head-long into the deep abyss below. The upper snow-slopes, too, were so steep that not even a goat, far less a man, could get over them. And he would have to pass below lofty walls and precipices whence avalanches of snow and vast masses of rocks were continually falling; and these would inevitably bury the intruder beneath their ruins. Moreover, a furious tempest continually swept the crown of the mountain, and the luckless adventurer, even if he wonderfully escaped the perils below, would be torn from the mountain and whirled through the air by this fearful blast. And the awful being upon the summit, who would surely punish the sacrilegious attempt to invade his sanctuary—who could hope to escape his vengeance? Many years ago, he continued, his grandfather, a great chief and warrior, and a mighty hunter, had ascended part way up the mountain, and had encountered some of these dangers, but he fortunately turned back in time to escape destruction; and no other Indian had ever gone so far.

Finding that his words did not produce the desired effect, he assured us that, if we persisted in attempting the ascent, he would wait three days for our return, and would then proceed to Olympia and inform our friends of our death; and he begged us to give him a paper (a written note) to take to them, so that they might believe his story. Sluiskin's manner during this harangue was earnest in the extreme, and he was undoubtedly sincere in his forebodings. After we had retired to rest, he kept up a most dismal chant, or dirge, until late in the night. The dim, white, spectral mass towering so near, the roar of the torrents below us, and the occasional thunder of avalanches, several of which fell during the night, added to the weird effect of Sluiskin's song.

The next morning we moved two miles farther up the ridge and made camp in the last clump of trees, quite within the limit of perpetual snow. Thence, with snow-spikes upon our feet and Alpine staff in hand, we went up the snow-fields to reconnoiter the best line of ascent. We spent four hours, walking fast, in reaching the foot of the steep, abrupt part of the mountain. After carefully scanning the southern approaches, we decided to ascend on the morrow by a steep, rocky ridge that seemed to lead up to the snowy crown.

Our camp was pitched on a high knoll crowned by a grove of balsam firs, near a turbulent glacial torrent. About nine o'clock, after we had lain down for the night, the firs round our camp took fire and suddenly burst out in a vivid conflagration. The night was dark and windy, and the scene—the vast, dim outlines of Takhoma, the white snow-fields, the roaring torrent, the crackling blaze of the burning trees—was strikingly wild and picturesque.

In honor of our guide we named the cascade at our feet Sluiskin's Falls; the stream we named Glacier Creek, and the mass of ice whence it derives its source we styled the Little Nisqually Glacier.

Before daylight the next morning, Wednesday, August 17, 1870, we were up and had breakfasted, and at six o'clock we started to ascend Takhoma. Besides our Alpine staffs and creepers, we carried a long rope, and ice-axe, a brass plate inscribed with our names, our flags, a large canteen, and some luncheon. We were also provided with gloves, and green goggles for snow-blindness, but found no occasion to use the latter. Having suffered much from the heat of the sun since leaving Bear Prairie, and being satisfied from our late reconnoissance that we could reach the summit and return on the same day, we left behind our coats and blankets. In three hours of fast walking we reached the highest point of the preceding day's trip, and commenced the ascent by the steep, rocky ridge already described as reaching up to the snowy dome. We found it to be a very narrow, steep, irregular backbone, being solid rock, while the sides were composed of loose broken rocks and débris. Up this ridge, keeping upon the spine when possible, and sometimes forced to pick our way over the loose and broken rocks at the sides, around columnar masses which we could not directly climb over, we toiled for five hundred yards, ascending at an angle of nearly forty-five degrees. Here the ridge connected, by a narrow neck or saddle, with a vast square rock, whose huge and distinct outline can be clearly perceived from a distance of twenty-five miles. This, like the ridge, is a conglomerate of basalt and trap, in well-defined strata, and is rapidly disintegrating and continually falling in showers and even masses of rocks and rubbish, under the action of frost by night and melting snow by day. It lies imbedded in the side of the mountain, with one side and end projected and overhanging deep, terrible gorges, and it is at the corner or junction of these two faces that the ridge joined it at a point about a thousand feet below its top. On the southern face the strata were inclined at an angle of thirty degrees. Crossing by the saddle from the ridge, despite a strong wind which swept across it, we gained a narrow ledge formed by a stratum more solid than its fellows, and creeping along it, hugging close to the main rock on our right, laboriously and cautiously continued the ascent. The wind was blowing violently. We were now crawling along the face of the precipice almost in mid-air. On the right the rock towered far above us perpendicularly. On the left it fell sheer off, two thousand feet, into a vast abyss. A great glacier filled its bed and stretched away for several miles, all seamed or wrinkled across with countless crevasses. We crept up and along a ledge, not of solid, sure rock, but one obstructed with the loose stones and débris which were continually falling from above, and we trod on the upper edge of a steep slope of this rubbish, sending the stones at every step rolling and bounding into the depth below. Several times during our progress showers of rocks fell from the precipice above across our path, and rolled into the abyss, but fortunately none struck us.

Four hundred yards of this progress brought us to where the rock joined the overhanging edge of the vast névé or snow-field that descended from the dome of the mountain and was from time to time, as pressed forward and downward, breaking off in immense masses, which fell with a noise as of thunder into the great canyon on our left. The junction of rock and ice afforded our only line of ascent. It was an almost perpendicular gutter, but here our ice-axe came into play, and by cutting steps in the ice and availing ourselves of every crevice or projecting point of the rock, we slowly worked our way up two hundred yards higher. Falling stones were continually coming down, both from the rock on our right and from the ice in front, as it melted and relaxed its hold upon them. Mr. Van Trump was hit by a small one, and another struck his staff from his hands. Abandoning the rock, then, at the earliest practicable point, we ascended directly up the ice, cutting steps for a short distance, until we reached ice so corrugated, or drawn up in sharp pinnacles, as to afford a foothold. These folds or pinnacles were about two or three feet high, and half as thick, and stood close together. It was like a very violent chop sea, only the waves were sharper. Up this safe footing we climbed rapidly, the side of the mountain becoming less and less steep, and the ice waves smaller and more regular, and, after ascending about three hundred yards, stood fairly upon the broad dome of mighty Takhoma. It rose before us like a broad, gently swelling headland of dazzling white, topped with black, where the rocky summit projected above the névé. Ascending diagonally towards the left, we continued our course. The snow was hard and firm under foot, crisp and light for an inch or two, but solidified into ice a foot or less beneath the surface.

The whole field was covered with the ice-waves already described, and intersected by a number of crevasses which we crossed at narrow places without difficulty. About half-way up the slope, we encountered one from eight to twenty feet wide and of profound depth. The most beautiful vivid emerald-green color seemed to fill the abyss, the reflection of the bright sunlight from side to side of its pure ice walls. The upper side or wall of the crevasse was some twelve feet above the lower, and in places overhung it, as though the snow-field on the lower side had bodily settled down a dozen feet. Throwing a bight of the rope around a projecting pinnacle on the upper side, we climbed up, hand over hand, and thus effected a crossing. We were now obliged to travel slowly, with frequent rests. In that rare atmosphere, after taking seventy or eighty steps, our breath would be gone, our muscles grew tired and strained, and we experienced all the sensations of extreme fatigue. An instant's pause, however, was sufficient to recover strength and breath, and we would start again. The wind, which we had not felt while climbing the steepest part of the mountain, now again blew furiously, and we began to suffer from the cold. Our course—directed still diagonally towards the left, thus shunning the severe exertion of climbing straight up the dome, although at an ordinary altitude the slope would be deemed easy— brought us first to the southwest peak. This is a long, exceedingly sharp, narrow ridge, springing out from the main dome for a mile into mid-air. The ridge affords not over ten or twelve feet of foothold on top, and the sides descend almost vertically. On the right side the snow lay firm and smooth for a few feet on top, and then descended in a steep, unbroken sheet, like an immense, flowing curtain, into the tremendous basin which lies on the west side of the mountain between the southern and northern peaks, and which is inclosed by them as by two mighty arms. The snow on the top and left crest of the ridge was broken into high, sharp pinnacles, with cracks and fissures extending to the rocks a few feet below. The left side, too steep for the snow to lie on, was vertical, bare rock. The wind blew so violently that we were obliged to brace ourselves with our Alpine staffs and use great caution to guard against being swept off the ridge. We threw ourselves behind the pinnacles or into the cracks every seventy steps, for rest and shelter against the bitter, piercing wind. Hastening forward in this way along the dizzy, narrow, and precarious ridge, we reached at length the highest point. Sheltered behind a pinnacle of ice we rested a moment, took out our flags and fastened them upon the Alpine staffs, and then, standing erect in the furious blast, waved them in triumph with three cheers. We stood a moment upon that narrow summit, bracing ourselves against the tempest to view the prospect. The whole country was shrouded in a dense sea of smoke, above which the mountain towered two thousand feet in the clear, cloudless ether. A solitary peak far to the southeast, doubtless Mount Adams, and one or two others in the extreme northern horizon, alone protruded above the pall. On every side of the mountain were deep gorges falling off precipitously thousands of feet, and from these the thunderous sound of avalanches would rise occasionally. Far below were the wide-extended glaciers already described. The wind was now a perfect tempest, and bitterly cold; smoke and mist were flying about the base of the mountain, half hiding, half revealing its gigantic outlines; and the whole scene was sublimely awful.

It was now five P.M. We had spent eleven hours of unremitted toil in making the ascent, and, thoroughly fatigued, and chilled by the cold, bitter gale, we saw ourselves obliged to pass the night on the summit without shelter or food, except our meagre lunch. It would have been impossible to descend the mountain before nightfall, and sure destruction to attempt it in darkness. We concluded to return to a mass of rocks not far below, and there pass the night as best we could, burrowing in the loose débris.

The middle peak of the mountain, however, was evidently the highest, and we determined to first visit it. Retracing our steps along the narrow crest of Peak Success, as we named the scene of our triumph, we crossed an intervening depression in the dome, and ascended the middle peak, about a mile distant and two hundred feet higher than Peak Success. Climbing over a rocky ridge which crowns the summit, we found ourselves within a circular crater two hundred yards in diameter, filled with a solid bed of snow, and inclosed with a rim of rocks projecting above the snow all around. As we were crossing the crater on the snow, Van Trump detected the odor of sulphur, and the next instant numerous jets of steam and smoke were observed issuing from the crevices of the rocks which formed the rim on the northern side. Never was a discovery more welcome! Hastening forward, we both exclaimed, as we warmed our chilled and benumbed extremities over one of Pluto's fires, that here we would pass the night, secure against freezing to death, at least. These jets were from the size of that of a large steampipe to a faint, scarcely perceptible emission, and issued all along the rim among the loose rocks on the northern side for more than half the circumference of the crater. At intervals they would puff up more strongly, and the smoke would collect in a cloud until blown aside and scattered by the wind, and then their force would abate for a time.

A deep cavern, extending into and under the ice, and formed by the action of heat, was found. Its roof was a dome of brilliant green ice with long icicles pendent from it, while its floor, composed of the rocks and débris which formed the side of the crater, descended at an angle of thirty degrees. Forty feet within its mouth we built a wall of stones, inclosing a space five by six feet around a strong jet of steam and heat. Unlike the angular, broken rocks met with elsewhere, within the crater we found well-rounded bowlders and stones of all sizes worn as smooth by the trituration of the crater as by the action of water. Nowhere, however, did we observe any new lava or other evidences of recent volcanic action excepting these issues of steam and smoke. Inclosed within the rude shelter thus hastily constructed, we discussed our future prospects while we ate our lunch and warmed ourselves at our natural register. The heat at the orifice was too great to bear for more than an instant, but the steam wet us, the smell of sulphur was nauseating, and the cold was so severe that our clothes, saturated with the steam, froze stiff when turned away from the heated jet. The wind outside roared and whistled, but it did not much affect us, secure within our cavern, except when an occasional gust came down perpendicularly. However, we passed a most miserable night, freezing on one side, and in a hot steam-sulphur bath on the other.

The dawn at last slowly broke, cold and gray. The tempest howled still wilder. As it grew light, dense masses of driven mist went sweeping by overhead and completely hid the sun, and enveloped the mountain so as to conceal objects scarce a hundred feet distant. We watched and waited with great anxiety, fearing a storm which might detain us there for days without food or shelter, or, worse yet, snow, which would render the descent more perilous, or most likely impossible. And when, at nine A.M., an occasional rift in the driving mist gave a glimpse of blue sky, we made haste to descend. First, however, I deposited the brass plate inscribed with our names in a cleft in a large bowlder on the highest summit—a huge mount of rocks on the east side of our crater of refuge, which we named Crater Peak—placed the canteen alongside, and covered it with a large stone. I was then literally freezing in the cold, piercing blast, and was glad to hurry back to the crater, breathless and benumbed.

We left our den of refuge at length, after exercising violently to start the blood through our limbs, and, in attempting to pass around the rocky summit, discovered a second crater, larger than the first, perhaps three hundred yards in diameter. It is circular, filled with a bed of snow, with a rocky rim all around and numerous jets of steam issuing from the rocks on the northern side. Both craters are inclined—the first to the west, and the latter to the east with a much steeper inclination, about thirty degrees. The rim of the second crater is higher, or the snow-field inside lower, than that of the first, and upon the east side rises in a rocky wall thirty feet above the snow within. From the summit we obtained a view of the northern peak, still partially enveloped in the driving mist. It appeared about a mile distant, several hundred feet lower than the center peak, and separated from it by a deeper, more abrupt depression or gap than that separating Crater and Success peaks. Like the latter, too, it is a sharp, narrow ridge springing out from the main mountain, and swept bare of snow on its summit by the wind. The weather was still too threatening, the glimpses of the sun and sky through the thick, flying scud were too few and fugitive, to warrant us in visiting this peak, which we named Peak Takhoma, to perpetuate the Indian name of the mountain.

Our route back was the same as on the ascent. At the steepest and most perilous point in descending the steep gutter where we had been forced to cut steps in the ice, we fastened one end of the rope as securely as possible to a projecting rock, and lowered ourselves down by it as far as it reached, thereby passing the place with comparative safety. We were forced to abandon the rope here, having no means of unfastening it from the rock above. We reached the foot of the rocky ledge or ridge, where the real difficulties and dangers of the ascent commenced, at 1.30 P.M., four and a half hours after leaving the crater. We had been seven and a half hours in ascending from this point to the summit of Peak Success, and in both cases we toiled hard and lost no time.

We now struck out rapidly and joyfully for camp. When nearly there Van Trump, in attempting to descend a snowbank without his creepers, which he had taken off for greater ease in walking, fell, shot like lightning forty feet down the steep incline, and struck among some loose rocks at its foot with such force as to rebound several feet into the air; his face and hands were badly skinned, and he received some severe bruises and a deep, wide gash upon his thigh. Fortunately the camp was not far distant, and thither with great pain and very slowly he managed to hobble. Once there I soon started a blazing fire, made coffee, and roasted choice morsels of a marmot, Sluiskin having killed and dressed four of these animals during our absence. Their flesh, like the badger's, is extremely muscular and tough, and has a strong, disagreeable, doggy odor.

Towards the close of our repast, we observed the Indian approaching with his head down, and walking slowly and wearily as though tired by a long tramp. He raised his head as he came nearer, and, seeing us for the first time, stopped short, gazed long and fixedly, and then slowly drew near, eying us closely the while, as if to see whether we were real flesh and blood or disembodied ghosts fresh from the evil demon of Takhoma. He seemed both astonished and delighted to find us safe back, and kept repeating that we were strong men and had brave hearts: "Skookum tilicum, skookum tumtum." He expected never to see us again, he said, and had resolved to start the next morning for Olympia to report our destruction.

The weather was still raw and cold. A dense cloud overhung and shrouded the triple crown of Takhoma and made us rejoice at our timely descent. The scanty shelter afforded by the few balsam firs about our camp had been destroyed by the fire, and the situation was terribly exposed to the chilly and piercing wind that blew from the great ice-fields. Van Trump, however, was too badly hurt to think of moving that night. Heating some large stones we placed them at our feet, and closely wrapped in our blankets slept soundly upon the open ground, although we awoke in the morning benumbed and chilled.

We found many fresh tracks and signs of the mountain-sheep upon the snowfields, and hair and wool rubbed off upon rocks, and places where they had lain at night. The mountain-sheep of Takhoma is much larger than the common goat, and is found only upon the loftiest and most secluded peaks of the Cascade Range. Even Sluiskin, a skillful hunter and accustomed to the pursuit of this animal for years, failed to kill one, notwithstanding he hunted assiduously during our entire stay upon the mountain, three days. Sluiskin was greatly chagrined at his failure, and promised to bring each of us a sheep-skin the following summer, a promise which he faithfully fulfilled.

The glacial system of Takhoma is stupendous. The mountain is really the focal centre and summit of a region larger than Massachusetts, and the five large rivers which water this region all find their sources in its vast glaciers. They are the Cowlitz, which empties into the Columbia; the White, Puyallup, and Nisqually rivers, which empty into Puget Sound sixty, forty, and twelve miles respectively north of Olympia; and the Wenass, which flows eastward through the range and empties into the Yakima, which joins the Columbia four hundred miles above its mouth. These are all large streams from seventy to a hundred miles in length. The White, Puyallup, and Cowlitz rivers are each navigable for steamboats for some thirty miles, and like the Nisqually show their glacial origin by their white and turgid water, which indeed gives the former its name.

The southwestern sides of the mountain furnish the glaciers which form the sources of the Nisqually, and one of these, at Sluiskin's Falls, has been already described. The main Nisqually glacier issues from the deep abyss overhung by the vast rock along the face of which our route of ascent lay, and extends in a narrow and somewhat crooked canyon for two miles. The ice at its extremity rises in an abrupt wall five hundred feet high, and a noisy torrent pours out with great force from beneath. This feature is characteristic of every glacier. The main Cowlitz glacier issues from the southeast side, just to the right of our ridge of ascent. Its head fills a deep gorge at the foot of the eastern front or face of the great mass of rock just referred to, and the southern face of which overhangs the main Nisqually glacier. Thus the heads of these glaciers are separated only by this great rock, and are probably not more than half a mile apart, while their mouths are three miles apart. Several smaller glaciers serve to swell the waters of the Cowlitz. In like manner the glaciers from the western side form the Puyallup, and those from the northern and northwestern sides the White River. The principal White River glacier is nearly ten miles long, and its width is from two to four miles. Its depth, or the thickness of its ice, must be thousands of feet. Streams and rivulets under the heat of the sun flow down its surface until swallowed by the crevasses, and a lakelet of deep blue water an eighth of a mile in diameter has been observed upon the solid ice. Pouring down from the mountain, the ice by its immense weight and force has gouged out a mass upon the northeastern side a mile in thickness. The geological formation of Takhoma poorly resists the eroding power of these mighty glaciers, for it seems to be composed not of solid rock, but of a basaltic conglomerate in strata, as though the volcanic force had burst through and rent in pieces some earlier basaltic outflow, and had heaped up this vast pile from the fragments in successive strata. On every side the mountain is slowly disintegrating.

What other peak can offer to scientific examination or to the admiration of tourists fourteen living glaciers of such magnitude, issuing from every side, or such grandeur, beauty, and variety of scenery?

At daylight we broke up our camp at Sluiskin's Falls, and moved slowly, on account of Van Trump's hurt, down the ridge about five miles to Clear Creek, where we again regaled ourselves upon a hearty repast of marmots, or "raw dog," as Van Trump styled them in derision both of the viand and of the cookery. I was convinced from the lay of the country that Clear Creek flowed into the Nisqually, or was, perhaps, the main stream itself, and that the most direct and feasible route back to Bear Prairie would be found by following down the valley of these streams to the trail leading from the Nisqually to Bear Prairie. Besides, it was evidently impossible for Van Trump, in his bruised and injured state, to retrace our rough route over the mountains. Leaving him as comfortable as possible, with all our scanty stock of flour and marmots, sufficient to last him nearly a week in case of need, I started immediately after dinner, with Sluiskin leading the way, to explore this new route. The Indian had opposed the attempt strenuously, insisting with much urgency that the stream flowed through canyons impossible for us to traverse. He now gradually veered away from the course of the stream, until ere-long he was leading directly up the steep mountain range upon our former route, when I called him back peremptorily, and kept him in the rear for a little distance.

Traveling through open timber, over ground rapidly descending, we came at the end of two miles to where the stream is hemmed in between one of the long ridges or spurs from Takhoma and the high mountain-chain on the south. The stream, receiving many affluents on both sides, its clear waters soon discolored by the yeasty glacial torrents, here loses its peaceful flow, and for upwards of three miles rushes furiously down a narrow, broken, and rocky bed in a succession of falls and cascades of great picturesque beauty. With much toil and difficulty we picked our way over a wide "talus" of huge, broken granite blocks and bowlders, along the foot of a vast mountain of solid granite on the south side of the river, until near the end of the defile, then crossed the stream, and soon after encountered a still larger branch coming from the north, direct from Takhoma, the product, doubtless, of the glaciers on the southern and southwestern sides. Fording this branch just above its confluence with the other, we followed the general course of the river, now unmistakably the Nisqually, for about four miles; then, leaving it, we struck off nearly south through the forest for three miles, and emerged upon the Bear Prairie. The distance was about thirteen miles from where we left Van Trump, and we were only some six hours in traveling it, while it took seventeen hours of terribly severe work to make the mountain-route under Sluiskin's guidance.

Without his help on the shorter route, too, it would have taken me more than twice the time it did. For the manner in which, after entering the defile of the Nisqually, Sluiskin again took the lead and proceeded in a direct and unhesitating course, securing every advantage of the ground, availing himself of the wide, rocky bars along the river, crossing and recrossing the milky flood which rushed along with terrific swiftness and fury, and occasionally forcing his way through the thick timber and underbrush in order to cut off wide bends of the river, and at length leaving it and striking boldly through the forest to Bear Prairie, proved him familiar with every foot of the country. His objections to the route evidently arose from the jealousy so common with his people of further exploration of the country by the whites. As long as they keep within the limits already known and explored, they are faithful and indefatigable guides, but they invariably interpose every obstacle their ingenuity can suggest to deter the adventurous mountaineer from exposing the few last hidden recesses that remain unexplored.

Mr. Coleman was found safe in camp, and seemed too glad to see us to think of reproaching us for our summary abandonment. He said that in attempting to follow us he climbed up so precipitous a place that, encumbered with his heavy pack, he could neither advance nor recede. He was compelled, therefore, to throw off the pack, which rolled to the very bottom of the mountain, and being thus delivered of his necessary outfit, he was forced to return to camp. He had been unable to find his pack, but having come across some cricketer's spikes among his remaining effects, he was resolved to continue his trip to, and make the ascent of, Rainier by himself; he had just completed his preparations, and especially had deposited on top of the lofty mountain which overlooked the prairie two caches, or stores, of provisions.

At daylight next morning, Sluiskin, with his little boy riding one of his own ponies, himself riding our little calico-colored pack-horse, now well rested and saucy, started back for Van Trump, with directions to meet us at the trail on the Nisqually. A heavy, drizzling rain set in soon afterwards; Mr. Coleman, who had gone early to bring in the contents of his mountain-top caches, returned about noon with a very small bundle, and, packing our traps upon Sluiskin's other pony, we moved over to the rendezvous, pitched Coleman's large gum-sheet as a partial shelter, made a rousing fire, and tried to be comfortable. Late in the afternoon the pony set up a violent neighing, and in a few minutes Van Trump, and Sluiskin with his little boy behind him, rode up, drenched to the skin. By following the bed of the river, frequently crossing and recrossing, the Indian had managed to ride to the very foot of the

Nisqually defile, when, leaving the horses in this boy's care, he hastened to Van Trump and carefully led and assisted him down. Despite the pain of his severe hurts, the latter was much amused at Sluiskin's account of our trip, and of finding Mr. Coleman safe in camp making tea, and for long after would repeat as an excellent joke Sluiskin's remark on passing the point where he had attempted to mislead me, "Skookum tenas man hiyu goddam."

We sent the horses back by the Indian to Bear Prairie for grass, there being no indications of the rain ceasing. The storm indeed lasted three days, during which we remained sheltered beneath the gum-sheet as far as possible, and endeavored to counteract the rain by heaping up our fire in front. About eight o'clock on the second morning, Sluiskin reported himself with our horse, which he returned, he said, because he was about to return to his lodge on the Cowlitz, being destitute of shelter and food for his family on Bear Prairie. He vigorously replenished the fire, declined breakfast, jeered Coleman for turning back, although probably the latter did not comprehend his broken lingo, and departed.

Sluiskin was an original and striking character. Leading a solitary life of hardships amidst these wilds, yet of unusual native intelligence, he had contrived, during rare visits to the settlements, to acquire the Chinook jargon, besides a considerable stock of English words, while his fund of general information was really wonderful. He was possessed of a shrewd, sarcastic wit, and, making no pretense to the traditional gravity of his race, did not scruple to use it freely. Yet beneath this he cherished a high sense of pride and personal independence. Although of the blood of the numerous and powerful Yakimas, who occupied the country just east of the Cascades, he disdained to render allegiance to them or any tribe, and undoubtedly regarded the superintendent of Indian affairs, or even the great father at Washington himself, with equally contemptuous indifference.

As the last rays of the sun, one warm, drowsy summer afternoon, were falling aslant the shady streets of Olympia, Mr. Longmire's well-worn family carry-all, drawn by two fat, grass-fed horses, came rattling down the main street at a most unusual pace for them; two bright flags attached to Alpine staffs, one projecting from each door, fluttered gayly overhead, while the occupants of the carriage looked eagerly forth to catch the first glimpse of welcoming friends. We returned after our tramp of two hundred and forty miles with visages tanned and sun-scorched, and with forms as lean and gaunt as greyhounds, and were received and lionized to the full, like veterans returning from an arduous and glorious campaign. For days afterward, in walking along the smooth and level pavements, we felt a strong impulse to step high, as though still striding over the innumerable fallen logs and boughs of the forest, and for weeks our appetites were a source of astonishment to our friends and somewhat mortifying to ourselves. More than two months had elapsed before Mr. Van Trump fully recovered from his hurts. We published at the time short newspaper accounts of the ascent, and, although an occasional old Puget Sounder will still growl, "They say they went on top of Mount Rainier, but I'd like to see them prove it," we were justly regarded as the first, and as I believe the only ones up to the present time, who have ever achieved the summit of Takhoma.

[1] Tak-ho'ma or Ta-ho'ma among the Yakimas, Klickitats, Puyallups, Nisquallys, and allied tribes of Indians, is the generic term for mountain, used precisely as we use the word "mount," as Takhoma Wynatchie, or Mount Wynatchie. But they all designate Rainier simply as Takhoma, or The Mountain, just as the mountain men used to call it the "Old He."

An Ascent of Long's Peak

ISABELLA LUCY BIRD

Long's Peak, 14,700 feet high, blocks up one end of Estes Park, and dwarfs all the surrounding mountains. From it on this side rise, snow-born, the bright St. Vrain, and the Big and Little Thompson. By sunlight or moonlight its splintered grey crest is the one object which, in spite of wapiti and bighorn, skunk and grizzly, unfailingly arrests the eye. From it come all storms of snow and wind, and the forked lightnings play round its head like a glory. It is one of the noblest of mountains, but in one's imagination it grows to be much more than a mountain. It becomes invested with a personality. In its caverns and abysses one comes to fancy that it generates and chains the strong winds, to let them loose in its fury. The thunder becomes its voice, and the lightnings do it homage. Other summits blush under the morning kiss of the sun, and turn pale the next moment; but it detains the first sunlight and holds it round its head for an hour at least, till it pleases to change from rosy red to deep blue; and the sunset, as if spell-bound, lingers latest on its crest. The soft winds which hardly rustle the pine needles down here are raging rudely up there round its motionless summit. The mark of fire is upon it; and though it has passed into a grim repose, it tells of fire and upheaval as truly, though not as eloquently, as the living volcanoes of Hawaii. Here under its shadow one learns how naturally nature worship, and the propitiation of the forces of nature, arose in minds which had no better light.

Long's Peak, "the American Matterhorn," as some call it, was ascended five years ago for the first time. I thought I should like to attempt it, but up to Monday, when Evans left for Denver, cold water was thrown upon the project. It was too late in the season, the winds were likely to be strong, etc.; but just before leaving, Evans said that the weather was looking more settled, and if I did not get farther than the timber line it would be worth going. Soon after he left, "Mountain Jim" came in, and said he would go up as guide, and the two youths who rode here with me from Longmount and I caught at the proposal. Mrs. Edwards at once baked bread for three days, steaks were cut from the steer which hangs up conveniently, and tea, sugar, and butter were benevolently added. Our picnic was not to be a luxurious or "well-found" one, for, in order to avoid the expense of a pack mule, we limited our luggage to what our saddle horses could carry. Behind my saddle I carried three pair of camping blankets and a quilt, which reached to my shoulders. My own boots were so much worn that it was painful to walk, even about the park, in them, so Evans had lent me a pair of his hunting boots, which hung to the horn of my saddle. The horses of the two young men were equally loaded, for we had to prepare for many degrees of frost. Jim was a shocking figure; he had on an old pair of high boots, with a baggy pair of old trousers made of deer hide, held on by an old scarf tucked into them; a leather shirt, with three or four ragged unbuttoned waistcoats over it; an old smashed wideawake, from under which his tawny, neglected ringlets hung; and with his one eye, his one long spur, his knife in his belt, his revolver in his waistcoat pocket, his saddle covered with an old beaver skin, from which the paws hung down; his camping blankets behind him, his rifle laid across the saddle in front of him, and his axe, canteen, and other gear hanging to the horn, he was as awful-looking a ruffian as one could see. By way of contrast he rode a small Arab mare, of exquisite beauty, skittish, high-spirited, gentle, but altogether too light for him, and he fretted her incessantly to make her display herself.

Heavily loaded as all our horses were, Jim started over the half-mile of level grass at a hard gallop, and then throwing his mare on her haunches, pulled up alongside of me, and with a grace of manner which soon made me forget his appearance, entered into a conversation which lasted for more than three hours, in spite of the manifold checks of fording streams, single file, abrupt ascents and descents, and other incidents of mountain travel. The ride was one series of glories and surprises, of "park" and glade, of lake and stream, of mountains on mountains, culminating in the rent pinnacles of Long's Peak, which looked yet grander and ghastlier as we crossed an attendant mountain 11,000 feet high. The slanting sun added fresh beauty every hour. There were dark pines against a lemon sky, grey peaks reddening and etherealizing, gorges of deep and infinite blue, floods of golden glory pouring through canyons of enormous depth, an atmosphere of absolute purity, an occasional foreground of cottonwood and aspen flaunting in red and gold to intensify the blue gloom of the pines, the trickle and murmur of streams fringed with icicles, the strange *sough* of gusts moving among the pine tops—sights and sounds not of the lower earth, but of the solitary, beast-haunted, frozen upper altitudes. From the dry, buff grass of Estes Park we turned off up a trail on the side of a pine-hung gorge, up a steep pine-clothed hill, down to a small valley, rich in fine, sun-cured hay about eighteen inches high, and enclosed by high mountains whose deepest hollow contains a lily-covered lake, fitly named "The Lake of the Lilies." Ah, how magical its beauty was, as it slept in silence, while *there* the dark pines were mirrored motionless in its pale gold, and *here* the great white lily cups and dark green leaves rested on amethyst-colored water!

From this we ascended into the purple gloom of great pine forests which clothe the skirts of the mountains up to a height of about 11,000 feet, and from their chill and solitary depths we had glimpses of golden atmosphere and rose-lit summits, not of "the land very far off," but of the land nearer now in all its grandeur, gaining in sublimity by nearness—glimpses, too, through a broken vista of purple gorges, of the illimitable Plains lying idealized in the late sunlight, their baked, brown expanse transfigured into the likeness of a sunset sea rolling infinitely in waves of misty gold.

We rode upwards through the gloom on a steep trail blazed through the forest, all my intellect concentrated on avoiding being dragged off my horse by impending branches, or having the blankets badly torn, as those of my companions were, by sharp dead limbs, between which there was hardly room to pass—the horses breathless, and requiring to stop every few yards, though their riders, except myself, were afoot. The gloom of the dense, ancient, silent forest is to me awe inspiring. On such an evening it is soundless, except for the branches creaking in the soft wind, the frequent snap of decayed timber, and a murmur in the pine tops as of a not distant waterfall, all tending to produce *eeriness* and a sadness "hardly akin to pain." There no lumberer's axe has ever rung. The trees die when they have attained their prime, and stand there, dead and bare, till the fierce mountain winds lay them prostrate. The pines grew smaller and more sparse as we ascended, and the last stragglers wore a tortured, warring look. The timber line was passed, but yet a little higher a slope of mountain meadow dipped to the south-west towards a bright stream trickling under ice and icicles, and there a grove of the beautiful silver spruce marked our camping ground. The trees were in miniature, but so exquisitely arranged that one might well ask what artist's hand had planted them, scattering them here, clumping them there, and training their slim spires towards heaven. Hereafter, when I call up memories of the glorious, the view from this camping ground will come up. Looking east, gorges opened to the distant Plains, then fading into purple grey. Mountains with pine-clothed skirts rose in ranges, or, solitary, uplifted their grey summits, while close behind, but nearly 3,000 feet above us, towered the bald white crest of Long's Peak, its huge precipices red with the light of a sun long lost to our eyes. Close to us, in the caverned side of the Peak, was snow that, owing to its position, is eternal. Soon the afterglow came on, and before it faded a big half-moon hung out of the heavens, shining through the silver blue foliage of the pines on the frigid background of snow, and turning the whole into fairyland. A courageous Denver artist attempted the ascent just before I arrived, but, after camping out at the timberline for a week, was foiled by the perpetual storms, and was driven down again, leaving some very valuable apparatus about 3,000 feet from the summit.

Unsaddling and picketing the horses securely, making the beds of pine shoots, and dragging up logs for fuel, warmed us all. Jim built up a great fire, and before long we were all sitting around it at supper. It didn't matter much that we had to drink our tea out of the battered meat tins in which it was boiled, and eat strips of beef reeking with pine smoke without plates or forks.

"Treat Jim as a gentleman and you'll find him one," I had been told; and though his manner was certainly bolder and freer than that of gentlemen generally, no imaginary fault could be found. He was very agreeable as a man of culture as well as a child of nature; the desperado was altogether out of sight. He was very courteous and even kind to me, which was fortunate, as the young men had little idea of showing even ordinary civilities. That night I made the acquaintance of his dog "Ring," said to be the best hunting dog in Colorado, with the body and legs of a collie, but a head approaching that of a mastiff, a noble face with a wistful human expression, and the most truthful eyes I ever saw in an animal. His master loves him if he loves anything, but in his savage moods ill-treats him. Ring's devotion never swerves, and his truthful eyes are rarely taken off his master's face. He is almost human in his intelligence, and, unless he is told to do so, he never takes notice of any one but Jim. In a tone as if speaking to a human being, his master, pointing to me, said, "Ring, go to that lady, and don't leave her again tonight." Ring at once came to me, looked into my face, laid his head on my shoulder, and then lay down beside me with his head on my lap, but never taking his eyes from Jim's face.

The long shadows of the pines lay upon the frosted grass, an aurora leaped fitfully, and the moonlight, though intensely bright, was pale beside the red, leaping flames of our pine logs and their red glow on our gear, ourselves, and Ring's truthful face. One of the young men sang a Latin student's song and two Negro melodies; the other, "Sweet Spirit, hear my Prayer." Jim sang one of Moore's melodies in a singular falsetto, and all together sang "The Star-spangled Banner" and "The Red, White, and Blue." Then Jim recited a very clever poem of his own composition, and told some fearful Indian stories. A group of small silver spruces away from the fire was my sleeping place. The artist who had been up there had so woven and interlaced their lower branches as to form a bower, affording at once shelter from the wind and a most agreeable privacy. It was thickly strewn with young pine shoots, and these, when covered with a blanket, with an inverted saddle for a pillow, made a luxurious bed. The mercury at 9 P.M. was 12° below the freezing point. Jim, after a last look at the horses, made a huge fire, and stretched himself out beside it, but Ring lay at my back to keep me warm. I could not sleep, but the night passed rapidly. I was anxious about the ascent, for gusts of ominous sound swept through the pines at intervals. Then wild animals howled, and Ring was perturbed in spirit about them. Then it was strange to see the notorious desperado, a red-handed man, sleeping as quietly as innocence sleeps. But, above all, it was exciting to lie there, with no better shelter than a bower of pines, on a mountain 11,000 feet high, in the very heart of the Rocky Range, under twelve degrees of frost, hearing sounds of wolves, with shivering stars looking through the fragrant canopy, with arrowy pines for bed-posts, and for a night lamp the red flames of a camp fire.

Day dawned long before the sun rose, pure and lemon colored. The rest were looking after the horses, when one of the students came running to tell me that I must come farther down the slope, for Jim said he had never seen such a sunrise. From the chill, grey Peak above, from the everlasting snows, from the silvered pines, down through mountain ranges with their depths of Tyrian purple, we looked to where the Plains lay cold, in blue-grey, like a morning sea against a far horizon. Suddenly, as a dazzling streak at first, but enlarging rapidly into a dazzling sphere, the sun wheeled above the grey line, a light and glory as when it was first created. Jim involuntarily and reverently uncovered his head, and exclaimed, "I believe there is a God!" I felt as if, Parsee-like, I must worship. The grey of the Plains changed to purple, the sky was all one rose-red flush, on which vermilion cloud-streaks rested; the ghastly peaks gleamed like rubies, the earth and heavens were new created. Surely "the Most High dwelleth not in temples made with hands!" For a full hour those Plains simulated the ocean, down to whose limitless expanse of purple, cliffs, rocks, and promontories swept down.

By seven we had finished breakfast, and passed into the ghastlier solitudes above, I riding as far as what, rightly or wrongly, are called the "Lava Beds," an expanse of large and small boulders, with snow in their crevices. It was very cold; some water which we crossed was frozen hard enough to bear the horse. Jim had advised me against taking any wraps, and my thin Hawaiian riding dress, only fit for the tropics, was penetrated by the keen air. The rarefied atmosphere soon began to oppress our breathing, and I found that Evans's boots were so large that I had no foothold. Fortunately, before the real difficulty of the ascent began, we found, under a rock, a pair of small overshoes, probably left by the Hayden exploring expedition, which just lasted for the day. As we were leaping from rock to rock, Jim said, "I was thinking in the night about your travelling alone, and wondering where you carried your Derringer, for I could see no signs of it." On my telling him that I traveled unarmed, he could hardly believe it, and adjured me to get a revolver at once.

On arriving at the "Notch" (a literal gate of rock), we found ourselves absolutely on the knifelike ridge or backbone of Long's Peak, only a few feet wide, covered with colossal boulders and fragments, and on the other side shelving in one precipitous, snow-patched sweep of 3,000 feet to a picturesque hollow, containing a lake of pure green water. Other lakes, hidden among dense pine woods, were farther off, while close above us rose the Peak, which, for about 500 feet, is a smooth, gaunt, inaccessible looking pile of granite. Passing through the Notch, we looked along the nearly inaccessible side of the Peak, composed of boulders and *débris* of all shapes and sizes, through which appeared broad, smooth ribs of reddish-colored granite, looking as if they upheld the towering rock mass above. I usually dislike bird's-eye and panoramic views, but, though from a mountain, this was not one. Serrated ridges, not much lower than that on which we stood, rose, one beyond another, far as that pure atmosphere could carry the vision, broken into awful chasms deep with ice and snow, rising into pinnacles piercing the heavenly blue with their cold, barren grey, on, on forever, till the most distant range upbore unsullied snow alone. There were fair lakes mirroring the dark pine woods, canyons dark and blue-black with unbroken expanses of pines, snow-slashed pinnacles, wintry heights frowning upon lovely parks, watered and wooded, lying in the lap of summer; North Park floating off into the blue distance, Middle Park closed till another season, the sunny slopes of Estes Park, and winding down among the mountains the snowy ridge of the Divide, whose bright waters seek both the Atlantic and Pacific Oceans. There, far below, links of diamonds showed where the Grand River takes its rise to seek the mysterious Colorado, with its still unsolved enigma, and lose itself in the waters of the Pacific; and nearer the snow-born Thompson bursts forth from the ice to begin its journey to the Gulf of Mexico. Nature, rioting in her grandest mood, exclaimed with voices of grandeur, solitude, sublimity, beauty, and infinity, "Lord, what is man, that Thou art mindful of him? or the son of man, that Thou visitest him?" Never-to-be-forgotten glories they were, burnt in upon my memory by six succeeding hours of terror.

You know I have no head and no ankles, and never ought to dream of mountaineering; and had I known that the ascent was a real mountaineering feat I should not have felt the slightest ambition to perform it. As it is, I am only humiliated by my success, for Jim dragged me up, like a bale of goods, by sheer force of muscle. At the Notch the real business of the ascent began. Two thousand feet of solid rock towered above us, four thousand feet of broken rock shelved precipitously below; smooth granite ribs, with barely foothold, stood out here and there; melted snow refrozen several times, presented a more serious obstacle; many of the rocks were loose, and tumbled down when touched. To me it was a time of extreme terror. I was roped to Jim, but it was of no use; my feet were paralyzed and slipped on the bare rock, and he said it was useless to try to go that way, and we retraced our steps. I wanted to return to the Notch, knowing that my incompetence would detain the party, and one of the young men said almost plainly that a woman was a dangerous encumbrance, but the trapper replied shortly that if it were not to take a lady up he would not go up at all. He went on to explore, and reported that further progress on the correct line of ascent was blocked by ice; and then for two hours we descended, lowering ourselves by our hands from rock to rock along a boulder-strewn sweep of 4,000 feet, patched with ice and snow, and perilous from rolling stones. My fatigue, giddiness, and pain from bruised ankles, and arms half pulled out of their sockets, were so great that I should never have gone halfway had not Jim, *nolens volens*, dragged me along with a patience and skill, and withal a determination that I should ascend the Peak, which never failed. After descending about 2,000 feet to avoid the ice, we got into a deep ravine with inaccessible sides, partly filled with ice and snow and partly with large and small fragments of rock, which were constantly giving way, rendering the footing very insecure. That part to me was two hours of painful and unwilling submission to the inevitable; of trembling, slipping, straining, of smooth ice appearing when it was least expected, and of weak entreaties to be left behind while the others went on. Jim always said that there was no danger, that there was only a short bad bit ahead, and that I should go up even if he carried me!

Slipping, faltering, gasping from the exhausting toil in the rarefied air, with throbbing hearts and panting lungs, we reached the top of the gorge and squeezed ourselves between two gigantic fragments of rock by a passage called the "Dog's Lift," when I climbed on the shoulders of one man and then was hauled up. This introduced us by an abrupt turn round the southwest angle of the Peak to a narrow shelf of considerable length, rugged, uneven, and so overhung by the cliff in some places that it is necessary to crouch to pass at all. Above, the Peak looks nearly vertical for 400 feet; and below, the most tremendous precipice I have ever seen descends in one unbroken fall. This is usually considered the most dangerous part of the ascent, but it does not seem so to me, for such foothold as there is is secure, and one fancies that it is possible to hold on with the hands. But there, and on the final, and, to my thinking, the worst part of the climb, one slip, and a breathing, thinking, human being would lie 3,000 feet below, a shapeless, bloody heap! Ring refused to traverse the Ledge, and remained at the "Lift" howling piteously.

From thence the view is more magnificent even than that from the Notch. At the foot of the precipice below us lay a lovely lake, wood embosomed, from or near which the bright St. Vrain and other streams take their rise. I thought how their clear cold waters, growing turbid in the affluent flats, would heat under the tropic sun, and eventually form part of that great ocean river which renders our far-off islands habitable by impinging on their shores. Snowy ranges, one behind the other, extended to the distant horizon, folding in their wintry embrace the beauties of Middle Park. Pike's Peak, more than one hundred miles off, lifted that vast but shapeless summit which is the landmark of southern Colorado. There were snow patches, snow slashes, snow abysses, snow forlorn and soiled looking, snow pure and dazzling, snow glistening above the purple robe of pine worn by all the mountains; while away to the east, in limitless breadth, stretched the green-grey of the endless Plains. Giants everywhere reared their splintered crests. From thence, with a single sweep, the eye takes in a distance of 300 miles—that distance to the west, north, and south being made up of mountains ten, eleven, twelve, and thirteen thousand feet in height, dominated by Long's Peak, Gray's Peak, and Pike's Peak, all nearly the height of Mont Blanc! On the Plains we traced the rivers by their fringe of cotton-woods to the distant Platte, and between us and them lay glories of mountain, canyon, and lake, sleeping in depths of blue and purple most ravishing to the eye.

As we crept from the ledge round a horn of rock I beheld what made me perfectly sick and dizzy to look at—the terminal Peak itself—a smooth, cracked face or wall of pink granite, as nearly perpendicular as anything could well be up which it was possible to climb, well deserving the name of the "American Matterhorn."[1]

Scaling, not climbing, is the correct term for this last ascent. It took one hour to accomplish 500 feet, pausing for breath every minute or two. The only foothold was in narrow cracks or on minute projections on the granite. To get a toe in these cracks, or here and there on a scarcely obvious projection, while crawling on hands and knees, all the while tortured with thirst and gasping and struggling for breath, this was the climb; but at last the Peak was won. A grand, well-defined mountain-top it is, a nearly level acre of boulders, with precipitous sides all round, the one we came up being the only accessible one.

It was not possible to remain long. One of the young men was seriously alarmed by bleeding from the lungs, and the intense dryness of the day and the rarefaction of the air, at a height of nearly 15,000 feet, made respiration very painful. There is always water on the Peak, but it was frozen as hard as a rock, and the sucking of ice and snow increases thirst. We all suffered severely from the want of water, and the gasping for breath made our mouths and tongues so dry that articulation was difficult, and the speech of all unnatural.

From the summit were seen in unrivalled combination all the views which had rejoiced our eyes during the ascent. It was something at last to stand upon the storm-rent crown of this lonely sentinel of the Rocky Range, on one of the mightiest of the vertebrae of the backbone of the North American continent, and to see the waters start for both oceans. Uplifted above love and hate and storms of passion, calm amidst the eternal silences, fanned by zephyrs and bathed in living blue, peace rested for that one bright day on the Peak, as if it were some region

> *Where falls not rain, or hail, or any snow,*
> *Or ever wind blows loudly.*

We placed our names, with the date of ascent, in a tin within a crevice, and descended to the Ledge, sitting on the smooth granite, getting our feet into cracks and against projections, and letting ourselves down by our hands, Jim going before me, so that I might steady my feet against his powerful shoulders. I was no longer giddy, and faced the precipice of 3,500 feet without a shiver. Repassing the Ledge and Lift, we accomplished the descent through 1,500 feet of ice and snow, with many falls and bruises, but no worse mishap, and there separated, the young men taking the steepest but most direct way to the Notch, with the intention of getting ready for the march home; and Jim and I taking what he thought the safer route for me—a descent over boulders for 2,000 feet, and then a tremendous ascent to the Notch. I had various falls, and once hung by my frock, which caught on a rock, and Jim severed it with his hunting knife, upon which I fell into a crevice full of soft snow. We were driven lower down the mountains than he had intended by impassable tracts of ice, and the ascent was tremendous. For the last 200 feet the boulders were of enormous size, and the steepness fearful. Sometimes I drew myself up on hands and knees, sometimes crawled; sometimes Jim pulled me up by my arms or a lariat, and sometimes I stood on his shoulders, or he made steps for me of his feet and hands, but at six we stood on the Notch in the splendor of the sinking sun, all colour deepening, all peaks glorifying, all shadows purpling, all peril past.

Jim had parted with his *brusquerie* when we parted from the students, and was gentle and considerate beyond anything, though I knew that he must be grievously disappointed, both in my courage and strength. Water was an object of earnest desire. My tongue rattled in my mouth, and I could hardly articulate. It is good for one's sympathies to have for once a severe experience of thirst. Truly, there was

> *Water, water, everywhere,*
> *But not a drop to drink.*

Three times its apparent gleam deceived even the mountaineer's practiced eye, but we found only a foot of "glare ice." At last, in a deep hole, he suc-ceeded in breaking the ice, and by putting one's arm far down one could scoop up a little water in one's hand, but it was tormentingly insufficient. With great difficulty and much assistance I recrossed the "Lava Beds," was carried to the horse and lifted upon him, and when we reached the camping ground I was lifted off him, and laid on the ground wrapped up in blankets, a humiliating termination of a great exploit. The horses were saddled, and the young men were all ready to start, but Jim quietly said, "Now, gentlemen, I want a good night's rest, and we shan't stir from here to-night." I believe they were really glad to have it so, as one of them was quite "finished." I retired to my arbor, wrapped myself in a roll of blankets, and was soon asleep.

When I woke, the moon was high shining through the silvery branches, whitening the bald Peak above, and glittering on the great abyss of snow behind, and pine logs were blazing like a bonfire in the cold still air. My feet were so icy cold that I could not sleep again, and getting some blankets to sit in, and making a roll of them for my back, I sat for two hours by the camp-fire. It was weird and gloriously beautiful. The students were asleep not far off in their blankets with their feet towards the fire. Ring lay on one side of me with his fine head on my arm, and his master sat smoking, with the fire lighting up the handsome side of his face, and except for the tones of our voices, and an occasional crackle and splutter as a pine knot blazed up, there was no sound on the mountain side. The beloved stars of my far-off home were overhead, the Plough and Pole Star, with their steady light; the glittering Pleiades, looking larger than I ever saw them, and "Orion's studded belt" shining gloriously. Once only some wild animals prowled near the camp, when Ring, with one bound, disappeared from my side; and the horses, which were picketed by the stream, broke their lariats, stampeded, and came rushing wildly towards the fire, and it was fully half an hour before they were caught and quiet was restored. Jim, or Mr. Nugent, as I always scrupulously called him, told stories of his early youth, and of a great sorrow which had led him to embark on a lawless and desperate life. His voice trembled, and tears rolled down his cheek. Was it semi-conscious acting, I wondered, or was his dark soul really stirred to its depths by the silence, the beauty, and the memories of youth?

We reached Estes Park at noon of the following day. A more successful ascent of the Peak was never made, and I would not now exchange my memories of its perfect beauty and extraordinary sublimity for any other experience of mountaineering in any part of the world. Yesterday snow fell on the summit, and it will be inaccessible for eight months to come.

[1] Let no practical mountaineer be allured by my description into the ascent of Long's Peak. Truly terrible as it was to me, to a member of the Alpine Club it would not be a feat worth performing.

Success

HALFORD J. MACKINDER

eptember 10, Sunday. 7.30 a.m. Aneroid 23.28, temperature 44, wet bulb 43. The sun is shining in a clear sky. I set the barograph for the third time. 9 a.m., aneroid 23.25, temperature 62, wet bulb 54, clear sky. 9.30, left Camp XVIIIa. 10.45, reached the twist in the ridge, having shortly before taken a fifteen minutes rest. 12.10, reached the first considerable upper glade, which we left again at 12.45 after lunch. 2.15, arrived in Camp XX after another ten minutes halt.

Have just destroyed the following note with regard to my people. Sulimani has been six times in Kikuyu. General Mathews reduced the Zanzibar duty to four rupees a porter. The porters are to be paid in Zanzibar. I am to ask Mr. Boustead, on behalf of Mr. Sleeman, to see that they are sent to Zanzibar on return.

Camburn tells me that he wants us to shoot, if possible, the following animals which have been seen—(1) a white-breasted hawk, (2) a red partridge, (3) a red-tailed thrush, (4) a mountain leopard.

9 p.m. Aneroid 21.3, temperature 42, wet bulb 40. There was thunder this afternoon, with heavy clouds moving southward. The upper clouds were also going southward. There were a very few spots of rain. There was no cloud roof below us, but a haze; it is now quite clear.

September 11, Monday. 7.30 a.m., aneroid 21.34, 10 p.m., aneroid 21.29, temperature 63, wet bulb 54. Now and during the whole night there has been a strong south wind. The sky is clear, but the Kenya cloud is just beginning to appear over the west and south slopes. The cloud roof, ending in two tongues, has retreated somewhat further south than usual.

I sent Camburn down with two porters and valuables to join Saunders at Camp XVIIIa, and myself left with five porters at 11.20, going up. 12 noon, aneroid 20.95, halted for ten minutes in glade above Camp XX, but on the same ridge. I noticed that Sattima was visible, and that high above it there was an extensive long cloud, but below there was no cloud roof except for a few isolated masses at the right level over Kikuyu. There was, however, a good deal of haze. Where I stood a strong south wind was blowing, but the Kenya clouds immediately above me were moving from the north. They were also

exhibiting some whorling movements. 12.50, aneroid 20.4, halted for fifteen minutes. There is a fresh
south wind. The smoke on the Laikipian plain and
on the slopes of Sattima indicates a south-east wind
below, but in the Kenya cloud above me, after allowance has been made for whorling, there is noticeable
a decided general movement southward.

We came past the agglomerate crags by a slightly
different route, and I saw on the slope several
hundred feet below the crags a large angular mass
of agglomerate resting on several large rounded
boulders.

2 p.m., halt on the site of Camp XXI. Aneroid
20.18, temperature dry bulb 58, wet 42 dry 53. The
above readings were taken successively; it is clouding
over and rapidly chilling. Within ten minutes of the
first reading it began to hail. This was the beginning
of an hour's considerable fall, which rested snow-
like on all the rock ledges and in the shadow of the
grass tufts. My four porters, with their usual perver-
sity, had left their boots behind. None-the-less, with
a little persuasion, conveyed through Musa, they
marched without halting from Camp XXI to Camp
XXII. As we entered the Höhnel Valley I had noted
that the clouds from the north came really from the
north-east, but the hail was due to a sudden entry of
lower cloud from the south-east.

We reached Camp XXII at 5 p.m. The peaks were
again clear. What a beautiful mountain Kenya is,

very graceful, not stern, but, as it seems to me, with a cold feminine beauty. The head of the Teleki Valley with its ruddy cliffs, edged and lined with snow or hail, appeared more beautiful in to-night's sunset than ever before. Suddenly the sun must have sunk below the horizon, for the glow went and the whole seemed chilled in a moment and struck one with an arctic beauty. Later, the young moon gave it a third, less tangible, aspect.

César and Joseph arrived before this. They had cut their way up the Darwin glacier, but could not descend and had to return by the arête on which we had spent the night. They report ice so hard that twenty and thirty blows are needed to cut a step, and snow that is powdery, in reality fine hail. However, it appears that a traverse is possible from our arête below the eastern peak on to the next arête, and thence the glacier which we can see hanging from the gap between the two peaks should be accessible. César has, unfortunately, hurt his wrist, owing to the repeated shock of the hard ice. 9 p.m., aneroid 19.1, temperature 33, wet bulb 30. It is clear and calm.

September 12, Tuesday. 9.30 a.m. From a cloudless sky a cloud from the south-east has suddenly shot up over Kenya peak and spread in all directions except south-east. High above the summit other clouds spread over the sky, all from the south-east. Presently whorling sets in, due to the up valley drifts, each whorl commencing with a peculiar shooting movement of cloud, as though marking the arrival of a new wind component.

I am now becoming convinced that, whatever may have been the case when we first arrived, we have now a lower south-east and an upper north-east wind, both interfered with by the local wind from under the lee of the mountain, and by the upward and downward valley-guided day and night breezes, due to the warming and chilling of the mountain. 10 a.m., aneroid 19.03, temperature 53, wet bulb 45. 11 a.m., the five porters start down taking with them one tent. They are to meet Saunders at Camp XX, and help him carry all the goods to the fort which he is to construct in the forest at Camp XVIIIa.

César, Joseph, and I were thus left alone. We started from Camp XXII at noon. The clouds were gathering in the head of the valley above us. By 1 p.m. we were half way up the terminal moraine of the Lewis glacier. There were many dead and some living tree groundsel on the lower end of this moraine. About 2 p.m., when we were on the south lateral moraine, beside the crevassed and falling part of the glacier, we were shut in by the cloud with occasional hail-stones. The wind was light, blowing up the valley.

We continued up the south lateral moraine for an hour, and then crossed the Lewis Glacier to the couloir at its north-west hand. We ascended the snow in the couloir for a little, and so gained the top of the talus to the left, which lies at the foot of the eastern face of the great south arête. Here we halted prior to climbing the face. The surface was at first rather steep, then flatter. It was covered with crisp new snow, and had a few narrow crevasses. The cloud had gradually risen from the glacier, and we could see our track across the white expanse. There was still an occasional hail-stone.

On the rock face were three *mauvais pas,* two traverses and a direct ascent of perhaps thirty feet. Our chief difficulty was in the loose condition of the stone, which was very hard and full of rectangular crystals. The jointing was into blocks, many of them overhanging. By 5.30 p.m. we had climbed almost to the top of the arête, and were pitching our little Mummery tent by means of our ice axes in a very convenient rock niche high above the Lewis Glacier.

The air cleared at the unusually late hour of 7 p.m. The temperature was then 32.5°. We took a little soup, and lay down. The night was calm, but our bed on the rock was damp and very hard. We had just room under our little shelter to lie side by side like sardines, and are stiff and cold-footed.

The following morning—Wednesday the 13th September—we were up at earliest dawn. The sky was clear above, but below to east and south was the cloud roof with a dark gulf beyond, probably the Tana Valley. The eastern horizon was lost in a mist of indescribably magnificent purples and reds, a vast abyss of mere colour. The temperature at 6 a.m. was 28°.

We were away upward just as the sun showed over the horizon, giving us a grateful touch of warmth. Soon we reached the site of our previous bivouac on the crest of the arête. Then we descended on to the ice slope beyond, traversing by steps the top of the Darwin Glacier, and so came to the arête which divides the head of that glacier. Here a biscuit tin marked the turning point of the reconnaissance made two days before by César and Joseph. They had ascended by the north side of the Lewis terminal moraine, had passed through the gap in the arête below the Lion's Tooth, had crossed the Darwin Glacier to the foot of the middle arête, and then worked up the ice beside the rock. The surface was very hard and steep, had an inch or two of snow upon it, and snow was falling, so that they decided not to attempt to descend by the way that they had come, but traversed the top of the glacier to the southern arête, and came home by our former path on the Lewis Glacier.

We now followed the arête above the biscuit tin. It would have guided us to the lesser summit, and from this we hoped to cross by the col to the greater. But after half an hour it became too steep to climb, and we were obliged to drop on to the hanging glacier to our left, which depended from the col between the summits. To cut steps across the glacier to the higher summit was the only way left to us.

The clouds at this moment—8.30 a.m.—compelled our attention. To south and west below us was the level fleecy surface of the cloud roof, and no doubt also to the east, but that side was still hidden by the southern arête. On the south this cloud was held close to the mountain by the south-east wind, so that the forest girdle was there covered, but on the west the cloud edge stood away from the slope, so that the dark forested descent was visible through the interval, and even a strip of the brown Laikipian plain at the mountain foot. Above the roof, but still below us, cloud came driving southward along the western slope, and then turning south eastward crossed the heads of the Höhnel and neighbouring valleys obliquely. Presently a cloud tongue shot southward from the east of the pink, and turning inward met the other stream, and the two whorled spirally upward, forming a huge threatening column towering above us to the south-west, but the peak was still sharply defined against the blue sky overhead.

It took three hours to cut our way across the hanging glacier to the further side of the gap between the two summits. At first we traversed the ice obliquely upward, each step requiring thirty blows with the axe. There was a thin covering of snow. Then we turned a little towards the base of the lesser summit, but seeing no foothold on the rock we resumed our oblique traverse upward towards the greater. The glacier was steep, so that our shoulders were close to it. Had we fallen, we should have gone over an ice cliff on to the Darwin Glacier several hundred feet below.

At last we reached the stone again, and almost exactly at noon set foot on the summit, which is like a low tower rising out of a heap of ruin, for the lichen-covered rock is vertically and horizontally jointed. On the top were two or three little turrets close together, and on these we sat. A small platform, a few feet lower, adjoined the south-eastern corner of the crag, and from this I got the shots with my Kodak of the summit with César and Joseph upon it.

I read the aneroid twice, throwing it out of gear between the readings, which showed 16.9 and 16.89 inches of pressure. The boiling point was 181.6° and the temperature with the swing thermometer 40°F. There was a light N.N.E. wind. The second peak bore 135° Magnetic, and we estimated that it was about thirty feet lower than that on which we stood. I broke off a fragment of the highly crystalline rock. The delay on the glacier had allowed the mid-day cloud to gather around the peak, but it was not thick. The sun shone through from above, and there were great rifts in the drifting mist through which we looked down on to the glaciers and arêtes beneath and away beyond into the radiant valleys. We remained about forty minutes at the top.

Then we scrambled down into the col between the peaks. The temptation was great to make an attempt on the second of them, for the way from the col did not appear difficult, but a storm was threatening, and we were not prepared to spend a second night on the mountain. We therefore descended over the hanging glacier, clearing the freshly fallen snow from the steps we had cut. By 6 p.m. we had reached our resting place of the previous night. There were still the three *mauvais pas* to be negotiated on the face of the arête, but we continued down by the light of the half moon and the sheen from the glacier below, throwing most of our goods over the cliff beforehand. It was not until 8.20—for we were tired—that we set foot on the Lewis Glacier, and not until 10.20 that we arrived in Camp XXII, hungry and weary, but triumphant.

The light effects were wonderful that evening. On the hanging glacier we had frequently been enveloped in thin cloud which shielded us from the equatorial sun, but at sunset we came again into clear air on the top of the southern arête. All the eastern horizon was glorious with a deep purple belt rising like a wall from the end of the landscape. Three hours later as we trudged home over the Lewis Glacier the great features of the mountain stood out as though boldly sketched in black and white crayons. The upper end of the glacier rose in snowy billows to the point of Lenana on the one hand, and on the other skirted the foot of the cliff by which we had descended, now black in the shadow cast by the moon. Below was the white expanse of the cloud roof, floating dreamily beside the solid texture of the ice. Most striking of all were the sheens and jetty blacks on the pinnacles of the Lion's Tooth and its lower neighbour.

The midnight scene as we supped by the camp fire was one never to be forgotten. The sound of the Nairobi river, swelling suddenly from time to time as the breeze changed, and even the occasional hoot of an owl made no break in the silence of the great peak standing brown and white in the glare of the setting moon. The Pleiades twinkled over the centre of the Lewis Glacier, while overhead the stars in the black vault were steady and without twinkle. Our camp was on the broad floor of a deep valley shut in by steep slopes to north and south, by the moraine of great blocks and tree groundsel on the west, by the red cliffs to the east, and by the cleft peak itself to the north-east. Those evenings, this the most wonderful of them all, were spent monosyllabically, warming our hands and feet at the fire, amid the mysterious shadows of the tree groundsel and the white gleams of the creeping groundsel. Our thoughts and rare words were divided between our conquest and the red cinders which spoke of home, until presently the scene around would break silently into our dreams, compelling our worship. Then as the fire dulled and our feet grew chilly the bark of a leopard ranging the hillside opposite would remind us of the early rise on the morrow, and with a drink of the cold water from our camp spring we rolled ourselves in our blankets without undressing, for warmth could not be wasted at Camp XXII.

Mount Assiniboine

JAMES OUTRAM

Three chief causes have combined to bring Mt. Assiniboine into special prominence among the peaks of Canada. First, its remarkable resemblance from certain aspects to the world-famed Matterhorn; though perhaps the Dent Blanche is more nearly its prototype in the better-known Swiss Alps. Secondly, the exquisite photographs and fascinating descriptions of Mr. W. D. Wilcox, the principal explorer of that region and the mountain's earliest biographer. And, lastly, the fact that it has repelled more assaults by mountain-climbers than any other peak in the Canadian Rockies, and gained a reputation at one time of extreme difficulty or even inaccessibility.

Its massive pyramid forms a conspicuous landmark from almost every considerable eminence for scores of miles around, towering fully 1500 feet above its neighbours, and by its isolation no less than by its splendid outline commanding attention and admiration.

It enjoys the proud distinction of being the loftiest mountain south of the railroad, 11,860 feet above sea-level, and is situated on the Continental watershed; and its mighty mass, with five huge spurs, covers an area of some thirty square miles and harbours fully a dozen picturesque lakes within the shelter of its giant arms.

The peak is grandest from its northern side. It rises, like a monster tooth, from an entourage of dark cliff and gleaming glacier, 5000 feet above the valley of approach; the magnificent triangular face, barred with horizontal belts of perpendicular cliff and glistening expanses of the purest snow and ice, which constitutes the chief glory of the mountain, soaring more than 3000 feet directly from the glacier that sweeps its base. On the eastern and the southern sides the walls and buttresses are practically sheer precipices 5000 to 6000 feet in vertical height, but the contour and character of the grand northern face more than compensate for the less sheer and lofty precipices.

The mighty monolith was named in 1885 by Dr. G. M. Dawson, of the Dominion Geological Survey, from a tribe of Indians inhabiting the plains, but he and his party only viewed it from afar. The first white men to explore the immediate vicinity, so far

as can be learned, were Messrs. R. L. Barrett and
T. E. Wilson, who, in 1893, made an expedition to
the mountain's base. The latter is a famous pioneer
of the Canadian Rockies, with probably a greater
knowledge of them than any man has ever yet possessed, and his store of yarns, drawn almost entirely
from personal experience or that of his immediate
associates, is as full of interest and valuable information as it is extensive. He and Mr. Barrett crossed the
Simpson Pass and followed down the Simpson River
to the mouth of a tributary flowing straight from
the direction of Mt. Assiniboine. Ascending this
with infinite difficulty, they crossed over to the
North Fork of the Cross River and thence upward
to their goal.

The ensuing summer Mr. S. E. S. Allen visited the
northern side by the same route, and the next year
both Mr. Allen and Mr. Barrett again succumbed to
the fascinations of the neighbourhood and were
found once more encamped under the shadow of
the monarch of the southern Rockies. The latter
traveller was accompanied by Mr. J. F. Porter and
Mr. W. D. Wilcox, who made some careful observations for altitude, and has given us a charming and
instructive description of his wanderings in his mag-
nificently illustrated book, "The Rockies of Canada."
Messrs. Barrett and Wilcox with Bill Peyto completed the circuit of the mountain on foot, a laborious but interesting undertaking which occupied them

a fraction more than two days. Beautiful valleys, heading in glaciers and adorned with lakes, alternated with rough and precipitous intervening ridges, each in turn having to be crossed. A large portion of the first day was spent traversing a valley devastated by a huge forest fire; the denseness of the charred and fallen trunks, sometimes piled ten or twelve feet above the ground, rendered progress painfully slow and toilsome, and, on emerging "black as coalheavers from our long walk in the burnt timber, seeking a refuge in the rocky ledges of the mountains, and clad in uncouth garments torn and discoloured, we must," writes Mr. Wilcox, "have resembled the aboriginal savages of this wild region."[1] Finally, by following a tiny goat track, discovered on the face of a dangerous-looking ridge, they reached the valley of the North Fork of the Cross River, falling in with Messrs. Smith and Allen, encamped in that pleasant spot and bent on similar investigations, and early next morning regained their camp on the shore of Lake Assiniboine.

Amongst the many valuable results of this complete inspection of the *massif* from every point of the compass, much information appealing particularly to the mountaineer was obtained. The contour of the main peak was shown to be very different from the symmetrical cone anticipated by the view from the north; the previously hidden southern ridge was found to extend a considerable distance at a comparatively easy angle to an abrupt and absolutely vertical precipice, and broken only by a deep notch that transforms the southern extremity into a sharp subsidiary peak. The eastern face defies approach to the summit from that direction, as does the southern buttress, but the south-western side developed a more practicable line of ascent and one that offered every prospect of success.

Not until 1899, however, was any attempt made to scale these attractive heights. That summer Mr. Wilcox returned to the neighbourhood accompanied by Mr. H. G. Bryant, of Philadelphia, well-known to those interested in Arctic exploration, and Mr. L. J. Steele, an Englishman. These two were the first to attack the formidable citadel, and narrowly escaped losing their lives in the attempt. They ascended the north-west *arête*[1] to an altitude of about 10,000 feet, when they were compelled to desist after several hours of hard climbing, an approaching storm assisting to hasten their descent. "They had just come to the top of the last ice slope, when Steele's foothold gave way, and he fell, dragging Bryant after him. There was but one possible escape from a terrible fall. A projecting rock of considerable size appeared not far below, and Steele, with a skilful lunge of his ice-axe, swung round to it and anchored himself in a narrow crevice, where the snow had melted away. No sooner had he come to a stop than Bryant shot over him from above and likewise found safety. Otherwise they would have fallen about six hundred feet, with serious, if not fatal, results."[2]

Another year went by, and a far more serious climbing expedition was fitted out to try to conquer the now famous mountain. Two brothers, the Messrs. Walling, of Chicago, with larger enthusiasm than experience in matters mountaineering, took with them three Swiss guides to force a way to the tantalizing summit. Camping, as usual, by the side of Lake Assiniboine, they followed Steele and Bryant's route to the northern glacier, ascending thence directly towards the apex by rock outcrops and snow-slopes. So far so good, though progress was extremely slow even on such an easy task; but when they came to the lowest belt of vertical cliffs the retreat was sounded and for the second time victory rested with Mt. Assiniboine.

On the return to Banff the shortest route (geographically) was taken, by White Man Pass and down the Spray Valley, but through some mismanagement or worse, the guides went on ahead, the Wallings were lost and, so the story goes, reduced to slaying a horse for sustenance before they were discovered by a search party. But the whole proceedings of the climb and the return were never very fully given to the public.

Thus far the north-west *arête* and the north face had been unsuccessfully approached, but Mr. Wilcox, mindful of the easier appearance of the south-western side, in 1901 made a determined effort to achieve victory from that direction. Mr. Bryant and two Swiss guides, E. Feuz and F. Michel, completed the party.

The main difficulty of this route was the approach to the mountain's base with a camping outfit, my more recent plan of access never having been deemed worthy of consideration as even entering the region of practicability. So eventually, after a long and toilsome march, they found themselves encamped in the deep gorge beneath the huge steep mass of the great peak. I shall have more to say concerning this side and their line of ascent later; suffice it now briefly to chronicle that, after attaining an altitude of 10,850 feet (just 1000 feet below the top), the avalanching appearance of the snow, the difficulties beyond, the lateness of the hour, and the over-burdening of Feuz (Michel having had an accident on the way out), combined to drive them back.

Thus the fortress still remained inviolate; the eastern side a precipice, the southern equally impossible, the northern and south-western faces, if possibly accessible, yet strongly guarded, each holding a record of an attack repelled. The *glacis* had proved too much for the first party of assailants, the solid rampart of the first line of fortifications beat back the next assault, and on the opener, more vulnerable side, alpine artillery had to be brought into play in order to defeat the last attempt. Who should be the next to storm the citadel and what the outcome?

This question was uppermost in many minds when the disappointing news of the last failure became known, and the pros and cons were most exhaustively debated around Mr. Whymper's camp-fire in the upper Yoho Valley, where I was having a glorious time amongst the untrodden peaks and glaciers of that delightful region. Peyto, our outfitter, Mr. Wilcox's companion on the circuit of Mt. Assiniboine six years before, added much fuel to the already consuming desire to examine and if possible ascend the mountain, but the distance and expense placed the enterprise beyond my reach, and I had sadly given up the whole idea when Peyto, asserting that for experienced mountaineers there was absolutely no question of a failure, pledged himself that if I would go and see and conquer he would undertake to get me there within two days from Banff and bring me back in less; and he proved even better than his word, although the journey had never previously been made in less than three days.

At the end of August, therefore, the weather being fine, though showing indications of the inevitable break which comes each year about this date, bringing a snowstorm to usher in the Indian summer of September, the opportunity arrived. It was "now or never" for this season, so I resolved to make a dash for the peak before the snow should render it impossible, and, Peyto being ready, a start upon the 31st was hastily arranged.

Thanks to the ready and able coöperation of Miss Mollison, the incomparable manager of the Hotel at Field, provisions, blankets, etc., were rapidly collected, and on the afternoon of the 30th Christian Häsler, Christian Bohren and I were in the train bound for Banff. Here we were met by Peyto and conducted to our tent pitched amongst the bushes near the bank of the Bow River. Our object was kept entirely secret, and scarcely a soul knew of the starting of the expedition at all.

The next morning was occupied in final arrangements, making up the packs and loading up, and eventually at half-past one the procession set out. First the cavalry; Bill Peyto, picturesque and workmanlike, led the way upon his trusty mare, then followed four pack-horses, the fastest and most reliable of Peyto's bunch, laden with tents, provisions, and our miscellaneous impedimenta; and Jack Sinclair, our assistant packer, also mounted, brought up the rear, to stimulate laggards and maintain the pace. Then came the infantry, comprising the two Christians and myself. Both the guides were tried companions, especially Häsler, who had already made several first ascents with me.

Mt. Assiniboine is only distant from Banff twenty miles in an air-line, yet by the shortest route it cannot be reached in twice that length of march; the trails are rough and often blocked with fallen timber, and no small amount of climbing is involved. But all of us were keen and determined each to do his best to make the journey to the base a record and the expedition a success.

The afternoon was sultry, with a haze about the summits and a look towards the west that boded rain; but the barometer stood well and hope was high.

At first we passed along the dusty road, with the cool, peaceful Bow eddying alongside, hemmed in by green banks, with overhanging branches dipping lazily in the current. Then we turned off into a winding trail that meandered among alders and small timber, with fallen logs and an occasional morass to vary the monotony. Close by, an eagle's nest hung in the branches of an isolated tree, the memorial of a domestic tragedy. Earlier in the summer Mr. Whymper had discovered it, had the two fine parent birds shot as specimens, each measuring over six feet from tip to tip of wing, and sent the baby to the aviary at Vancouver.

Behind us rose the impressive walls of Cascade Mountain; on our right, across the valley, the sharp pinnacles of Mt. Edith pierced the sky; and wooded slopes flanked us on the left and rose to the fine summit of Mt. Massive right in front.

Soon we reached Healy Creek where it emerges from a narrow gorge, and crossed its double stream, the pedestrians having to clamber up behind the horsemen to make the passage dryshod. Leaving the broad, level valley of the Bow, and with it every trace of civilization for some days to come, we plunged into the ravine beside the swift, translucent river, until we mounted a very steep trail through thick forest and emerged high above the creek in a fine valley whence the retrospective views were very beautiful.

Our path led through a tract of burned and fallen timber to more open ground, trending steadily towards Simpson Pass, above which stood a gabled mountain, with a small glacier cradled on its bosom, against a gloomy, ominous background of dark and lurid clouds. The valley narrowed before us, well wooded near the torrent-bed. On one side rugged summits rose abruptly from the thickly timbered slopes; on the other, the more open alps, interspersed with belts and groves of trees, bare cliffs and rocky terraces, merged into castellated peaks, the topmost crowned with snow.

As the evening shadows lengthened, before our camping-ground was reached, strong gusts of wind came sweeping down the gorge, with driving rain beating pitilessly in our faces, but we pressed on until we found a pretty and fairly sheltered spot among the woods, where we pitched our tents.

A busy scene ensues. Peyto and Sinclair unload and attend to the horses; the guides are energetically employed cutting and collecting fuel; fire and water, the opening of boxes and unpacking necessaries are my allotted share. In an incredibly short space of time the tents are up, the packs made snug, supper is ready, and we are all gathered round the blazing fire fully prepared to do ample justice to the bannocks and bacon and the huge saucepan full of steaming tea, under the black canopy of pines and almost darker sky.

Next morning we were off at half-past seven, in fair weather, though the trees and undergrowth were dripping. We crossed the stream and, after twenty minutes' gradual ascent, diverged from the main trail to Simpson Pass and followed a steep pathway to the south through thick firs up a narrow rocky canyon till we arrived in a beautiful open park. The carpet of luxuriant grass and mossy turf was sprinkled gayly, although September was upon us, with a wealth of flowers, dark groups of trees bordered the rich expanse and crowned the knolls that broke its surface here and there, and, on either hand, the green slopes, broken by picturesque rock outcrops, culminated in a line of rugged pinnacles.

The timber-line is passed soon after, and we mount steadily to a breezy, undulating alp, green and flower-strewn, skirting the Continental watershed, and bearing frequent pretty lakelets in the sheltered hollows. Ever and anon a deep gorge dips sharply towards the east or west, giving a glimpse of larger, wooded valleys, where Healy Creek and Simpson

River run to join the Bow and Kootenay, and finally sink to rest in the waters of the rival oceans.

This upland route was taken by Mr. Wilcox on his second journey to Mt. Assiniboine, and it is undoubtedly the finest way as well as probably the easiest and quickest, in spite of a terrific 1500 feet of descent to the source of the Simpson River.

About ten o'clock, from a lofty ridge some 2000 feet above our camp, we caught our first glimpse of our objective peak, bearing from this point a remarkable resemblance to the Swiss Dent Blanche as it loomed through the slight haze, fourteen or fifteen miles away, dwarfing all the other points and ranges. An hour later, from the highest point upon our highland trail, about 7700 feet above the sea, we obtained a still better view of the noble pyramid, towering above a blue-black ridge hung with white glaciers, which lay between us and its base.

Crossing and recrossing the "backbone of the Continent," we skirted the walls of an imposing natural fortification, fully 2000 feet in height, and, passing under its frowning ramparts close to the shores of two or three small lakes, halted for lunch near a round pond, from which some ducks flew off at our approach, and which from the numerous tracks leading into and out of it, we christened "The Bears' Bath-tub."

All this time the going had been good, and Peyto made the most of it, leading at a tremendous rate, with Sinclair driving on the pack-animals, we poor two-legged tramps having to do our utmost to keep pace with them.

After lunch a new experience began, where we in turn had a conspicuous advantage,—a tremendous drop (1500 feet in 55 minutes, pack-horse time) into an extraordinarily steep, weird valley, narrow and fire-swept, its serried ranks of bare and ghostly poles backed by slopes of scanty grass and a tumultuous expanse of rough gray rocks and tongues of scree. Towards the lower end an intricate maze of fallen logs was encountered, through which Peyto steered the horses with marvellous skill and rapidity, until we gained the valley of the chief source of the Simpson River, barren and boulder-strewn, divided into rugged sections by great ridges traversing it from side to side. Bare, burned trees reared their gaunt stems about us, or, fallen, littered the valley-bed, where strawberries and raspberries, gooseberries and blueberries, grew in wild profusion.

Crossing several of the strange barrier ridges, we soon arrived at the head of the valley, a *cul-de-sac*, with a grand amphitheatre of precipices and abrupt acclivities, 300 feet or more in height, blocking our way and towering above the rich green flat, on which we halted for a brief well-earned rest beside a tree-girt lakelet, fed by a fine cascade that leaped from the rim of the great cirque above.

A zigzag track conducted us to the lowest point of this imposing barrier, and a scene of indescribable bleakness burst upon our gaze. The sun was hidden by the gathering clouds and the leaden sky formed a fit background for the rock-bound basin at our feet, hemmed in by gray, ruined towers, from which wide belts and tapering tongues of tumbled scree streamed down among the bare poles of the stricken pines, with a tiny tarn, sombre and forbidding, in its depths.

It was a fitting prelude to the long valley on which we now entered. Here was the acme of sheer desolation. Green-gray rocks and stones were strewn and piled in wild confusion amid sparse, stunted pines and firs; crumbling, drab-coloured side-hills were lost in jagged, broken ridges and shattered pinnacles, that loomed in sullen dulness against the mournful sky, while a light drizzle bathed the scene in gloomy haze. Here and everywhere along the route the dreary silence and the strange scarcity of living things—a notable characteristic of the Canadian Cordilleras—were very striking. The whistle of the marmot, the rare whir of grouse, a hawk or eagle, and a little bird or two, with the occasional tracks of bear or deer, marten or mountain goat, alone betrayed that the region is not quite bereft of life.

Thus we swung on mile after mile, till the melancholy conditions began to change: grass and light undergrowth appeared, the clouds broke, and, as we neared a rocky lake, Mt. Assiniboine came into view once more, about five miles ahead, grander than ever, and, in spite of evening gloom, showing some detail of its horizontal belts of cliff and smooth, shining icy slopes.

Then came park country, rich green pasturage and dark forest belts, with a winding coal-black stream-bed meandering in the most abandoned manner through it all; and above, on either side, sharp, serrated ridges, severed by wide passes to the Spray and Cross Rivers, converged in the mass of Mt. Assiniboine.

Still on we tramp, weary but buoyed up by the knowledge that the goal is near. Darkness falls apace and

> "Far along
> From peak to peak, the rattling crags among,
> Leaps the live thunder! Not from one lone cloud,
> But every mountain now hath found a tongue."

A most impressive welcome from the still uncon-quered mountain, but more sinister than those whose hopes depended on fine weather quite appreciated.

At length, at 7.20, our chosen camping-ground was reached, sheltered by a grove of trees, beside a trickling rivulet with the dark waters of Lake Assini-boine just visible beyond.

This lake, one of a dozen or more that nestle close under the precipices of the giant peak, is nearly two

miles long, and, like many others in the neighbourhood, is without a visible outlet. The waters seem to
drain away through the loose limestone strata, and in
some valley far below suddenly burst forth from a
mysterious subterranean cavern, a full-grown stream.
This we were able to observe for ourselves at the
source of the main Simpson River, at the head of the
cul-de-sac, some miles from the nearest body of water
at a higher altitude sufficient to produce so large a
flow.

The night was none too promising—warm and
cloudy, with light showers at intervals and distant
muttering thunder; and, although later on the stars
came out, ominous clouds still hung heavy round the
horizon. The silence was broken again and again by
the rumble and crash of falling ice and stones from
the glacier a mile away, which aided the anxiety concerning weather prospects to drive the slumber from
our wearied frames.

Nevertheless we were early astir. The moon was
shining fitfully athwart the clouds and lighting up
our noble peak with silvery brightness. As the sun
rose, we had an opportunity of studying the mountain. Our camp, at an elevation of about 7200 feet,
lay near the shore of the lake, a long mile from the
cliff over which the northern glaciers of Mt. Assiniboine descend abruptly; 3000 feet above the glacier
rises the mighty monolith, a relic of the Carbonifer-
ous age. Two jagged ridges trend sharply upward

from the outlying spurs, until they meet in a dark rocky apex just below the glistening, snowy summit; between them lies the formidable northern face, set at a fearsome angle, and banded with almost horizontal strata, which form an impressive alternation of perpendicular cliff belts and glassy slopes of ice. The lowest band is specially remarkable—a spectacular, striated wall of brilliant red and yellow rock, running apparently entirely round the mountain, and particularly striking where the erosion and disintegration of the ridges leave a succession of coloured spires and pinnacles, radiant in the glowing sunshine.

By the advice of Peyto, the only member of the party who had ever been near the peak before, we determined to make our attempt from the south-western side; but, instead of taking the horses by the long and arduous route adopted by Mr. Wilcox and Mr. Bryant on the occasion of their last attack, I conceived the plan of crossing the outlying spurs at a high altitude on foot from the usual base camp, believing that some way, for practised mountaineers at least, could be discovered whereby the farther side might be reached and an open bivouac be made a starting-point next morning, if it proved too long or difficult a task to gain the summit in a single day.

Being wholly unaware of the character of the mountain on the hidden side, and anticipating considerable difficulty in getting to the south-western ridge, by which we hoped to reach the point where the last climbers were compelled to halt, we had little expectation of being successful on the first day, particularly as the nights were closing in at a comparatively early hour. So off we started at six o'clock,—Peyto, Häsler, Bohren and I—laden with two days' provisions, minor changes of raiment, blankets, and a light tent for the night, besides the usual camera and sundry other paraphernalia.

Twenty minutes' walk along the green flat brought us to the first snow, and a steep pull up hard snow-slopes and a craggy wall of rock, followed by an awkward scramble over loose *débris*, landed us at half-past seven on the ice above. The glacier, covered with congealed snow and thin moraine, stretched away before us at an easy angle, with the great peak towering aloft upon our left. As we moved rapidly along I took the opportunity to scan with interest and curiosity the peculiar characteristics of that remarkable face, but the result of my observations was locked securely in my breast, and not revealed until, on the following afternoon, we stood upon the crest above.

Forty minutes of quick walking took us to the summit of the sharp ridge which forms the sky-line to the west and merges in the main north-western *arête*. Two hundred feet below us lay another glacier, and away to our left a second pass, at the base of the great western ridge. Dropping down to the ice, we followed up the glacier, zigzagging to avoid the large *crevasses*, to the narrow little pass, which we reached at nine o'clock and found ourselves about 9600 feet above the sea and 2400 feet above the camp.

From this point the lower portion of the unknown side of our mountain lay in full view, and, to our joy, we saw that the anticipated difficulties were non-existent. A comparatively easy traverse, along narrow but ample ledges covered with snow and *débris*, across the ribs and stony gullies which seamed the south-western face, would bring us, with scarcely any loss of elevation, to the south-west ridge, whence the climb proper was expected to begin. Each of the gullies seemed to be a much-used channel for stones and ice and snow, and was of excessive steepness, so no inducement was offered to try an upward route nearer than the line that Mr. Wilcox took in his ascent from the valley. Below the horizontal ledge of the proposed traverse the mountain shelved steeply down in long expanses of loose stones and snow, with not a little ice, into the depths of the contracted valley far beneath, containing the inevitable lakelet.

To counteract, however, this piece of unexpected good fortune, the light fleecy clouds, which had been hovering over the lower western peaks and growing larger and denser every hour, were blotting out the view and soon enveloped us in their chill embrace. With little hope of a successful ascent, we nevertheless made our way to the ridge, where we *cached* our blankets, tent, and the bulk of the provisions, and, after a second breakfast, continued our upward progress at about half-past ten.

Our circle of vision dwindled from one hundred yards to fifty at the most; a steady drizzle, mingled with sleet, began to fall as we climbed cliff and ledge and gully, loose rocks and slopes of *débris*, as each appeared through the mists in front of us; and every few yards we built a little pile of stones to guide us in returning.

At length, at about 10,750 feet altitude, out of the gloom a mighty wall, seventy or eighty feet in height, loomed before us, its top lost in the clouds. The face seemed sheer, and actually overhung in places. None of us had ever seen this side of Mt. Assiniboine, excepting Peyto, who had left us a short distance below to prospect for minerals, and we knew not where the summit lay. Of course we went first in the wrong direction. Imagining that this belt was as unbroken here as on the northern face, we sought a cleft up which to clamber and skirted the base to the right till we were brought up by a tremendous precipice some 6000 feet in depth. We had suddenly reached the edge of a gigantic buttress, where its converging sides met at an abrupt angle. Before us, and on either hand, was empty space, and at our feet a seemingly unbroken drop thousands of feet deep.

Behind rose the sharp edge of rock like polished masonry. Below the stony ledge by which we had approached, the mountain-side shelved to the south in rugged steepness into far-distant gloom; and as we peered with caution round the angle, the farther side disclosed a most appalling face of black, forbidding precipice, one of the finest and most perpendicular it has been my lot to see.

Here for some moments I stood in solemn awe, perched like a statue in a lofty niche, cut in the topmost angle of a vast, titanic temple, with space in front, on either side, above, below, the yawning depths lost in the wreathing mists that wrapped the mountain's base.

Our progress in this direction barred, we now retraced our steps and spied a little rift by which, in spite of a fair overhang for the first twelve or fifteen feet, thanks to firm hand and foot holds, we were enabled to scramble to the summit of the cliff. Working to the left by a steep succession of ledges and clefts, we reached a narrow, broken ridge running upward from the west, with a sheer drop upon the farther side. We thought that we had struck the main western *arête* (for it is very difficult to locate one's self in a dense mist, especially upon an unknown mountain which we expected to find a regular three-sided cone) and followed its lead, till in ten minutes, to our great amazement, we found ourselves upon a *peak!* Narrow ridges descended to the east and west, the steep face of our ascent lay to the south, while upon the northern side a mighty precipice fell away virtually perpendicularly for thousands of feet, broken only by a short buttress, with equally sheer walls and edged with jagged pinnacles.

This "Lost Peak" was to us most mysterious. It seemed a genuine summit, narrow and pointed though it was, in altitude a trifle over 11,000 feet. Yet where upon the mass of Mt. Assiniboine was such a peak? We had imagined that the giant tooth rose more or less symmetrically on every side and judged the back ridge by the two that we had seen. Häsler at first insisted that we were on the veritable summit, but the elevation and configuration of our whole environment demolished such a theory. We strained our eyes; but, though the breeze kept the thick clouds in constant motion, we could not see more than about a hundred yards ahead. We shouted in this direction and in that; but our voices died away into space until at last held by some loftier mass, which echoed back an answer from the direction whence we had just come! Then we knew that we were standing upon the south-eastern ridge, which must be longer and less steep, at any rate in its upper portion, than any of the others, and possess a distinct minor peak, separated from the main summit by a considerable break.

Such proved to be the case. After an hour spent in the cold and wet, striving to pierce the clouds, hoping some stronger current of wind might waft them off, and thus enable us to see the top and give us some idea of its character and how we might approach it, we built a "stone man" to commemorate our visit, and, at half-past one, returned along the west *arête* until a chasm yawned beneath our feet—how deep we could not tell (it proved about 200 feet)—and forced us to descend by our cliff route and down the crack to the base of the big wall. A few minutes' going in the opposite direction brought us to a broad snow *couloir*, where the cliff receded and trended upward to the gap into which we had been gazing from above not long before, and away upon our left stretched the steep face of the great peak itself.

It was now too late to think of climbing farther, so we descended rapidly and rejoined Peyto near the *cache*. Here, during a meal, we held a council of war, and came to the unanimous determination to shoulder our packs and return to camp; feeling that, if the morrow were wet, we should be better off there, and if fine, it would take but little longer to come round in light marching order from the north than to make the ascent thus far with heavy packs from the tree-line. In spite of a very speedy return, night fell upon us before we had quite descended the cliff wall below the northern glacier, and we stumbled into camp in black darkness about a quarter-past eight.

The clouds had begun to dissipate towards sunset; later on the moon rose in a clear, star-spangled sky; and the chill of frost augured favourably for our second campaign.

September 3rd, a notable date for us and Mt. Assiniboine, dawned brilliantly. At ten minutes past six our little party of three set out from camp in the best of spirits, encouraged by the hearty good wishes of the packers; and made rapid progress by the route of the previous day. In two and a half hours we were on the second pass, enjoying this time a wide view to the south and the north-west of an expanse of indented mountain ranges and deep yawning valleys, with a little lake far below in every gorge. A brief halt here, and then on to the south-western ridge, reaching the *cache* three and a quarter hours from the start. Upward, past the coloured belt, to our great cliff of yesterday. There, at half-past ten, we turned off to the left and crossed the *couloir*, full of deep snow upon an icy basis.

Beyond it lay the final thousand feet of the great mountain, its steep and rugged face a series of escarpments broken by tiny ledges and occasional sharp pinnacles, and rent at distant intervals by clefts and crevices nearly vertical. Slopes of solid ice or ice-hard snow, demanding arduous step-cutting, intervened below each wall and ledge and filled each cavity. The rocks were very brittle and extremely insecure, and to the ordinary difficulties there was added that abomination of the mountaineer, *verglas*, the thin coating of ice upon the rocks from the night's frost after the rain and sleet of yesterday.

The general line was diagonally across the face, but frequent minor consultations were required, the problems of immediate procedure being numerous.

Steadily onward the little party made its cautious way across these difficult approaches: ever on the alert, hand and foot alike pressed into service; each hold fully tested before the weight was trusted to it. A slippery ledge demanded an ignominious crawl; a series of gymnastic efforts were required to surmount some of the straight-up rocks and buttresses, where holds were few and far between. Detours were frequent to avoid impossible conditions; all sorts of cracks and crevices had to be utilized; and icy rifts were sometimes the only avenues of access to the tops of smooth, unbroken cliffs.

Thus step by step the advance continued, till, after a final scramble up a gully lined with solid ice and almost as steep and narrow as a chimney, we stood triumphantly upon the south *arête*, the summit in full view not more than 300 feet above, reached by an easy ridge of snow, and Mt. Assiniboine we knew was ours.

The strangest feature of the ascent lay in the fact that now for the first time we saw the actual summit, as the cliffs rose so steeply during our approach that we could never see more than a short distance beyond us.

White, vaporous clouds had been slowly drifting up for the last hour, and, fearing a repetition of the previous day's experience and the loss of the view, we hurried to the top, pausing only for a few moments to enjoy the panorama, to renew our acquaintance with our "Lost Peak," now 500 feet below us, and to take a picture through the mist of the white summit, with its splendid eastern precipice.

A quarter of an hour sufficed to complete our victory, and at half-past twelve we stood as conquerors 11,860 feet above the sea (Government survey altitude from distant bases), on the loftiest spot in Canada on which a human foot had then been planted.

The summit is a double one, crowned with ice and snow, the two points rising from the extremities of an almost level and very narrow ridge 150 feet in length, at the apex of the sharp *arêtes* from north and south. On the western side snow-slopes tilted downward at a very acute angle, while on the east a stupendous precipice was overhung by a magnificent succession of enormous cornices from which a fringe of massive icicles depended.

One at a time—the other two securely anchored— we crawled with the utmost caution to the actual highest point, and peeped over the edge of the huge, overhanging crest, down the sheer wall to a great, shining glacier 6000 feet or more below.

The view on all sides was remarkable, although the atmosphere was somewhat hazy and unsuitable for panoramic photography. Perched high upon our iso-lated pinnacle, fully 1500 feet above the loftiest peak for many miles around, below us lay unfolded range after range of brown-gray mountains, patched with snow and sometimes glacier-hung, intersected by deep chasms or broader wooded valleys. A dozen lakes were counted, nestling between the outlying ridges of our peak, which proudly stands upon the backbone of the Continent, and supplies the head-waters of three rivers—the Cross, the Simpson, and the Spray.

Far away to the north-west, beyond Mt. Ball and the Vermilion Range, we could descry many an old friend among the mountains of the railway belt—Mt. Goodsir and the Ottertails, Mt. Stephen and Mt. Temple, with the giants of the Divide, Mts. Victoria, Lefroy, Hungabee, and a host of others, a noble group of striking points and glistening glaciers.

The main ridge northward, after a sharp descent of fifty feet, falls gently for a hundred yards or so, and then makes a wild pitch down to the glaciers at the mountain's base. When we arrived at this point (only through my most strenuous insistence, for the guides were anxious to return at once by the way we came), we looked down on the imposing face that is perhaps Assiniboine's most characteristic feature.

On the right the drop is perpendicular, a mighty wall with frequent overhanging strata and a pure snow curtain hanging vertically beneath the crown-ing cornice. But the north face, though not so sheer or awesome, is perhaps still more striking and unique. The shining steeps of purest ice, the encircling belts of time-eroded cliffs, sweep downward with tremendous majesty. Between the two a ragged ridge is formed, narrow and broken, like a series of roughly fractured wall-ends.

As we gazed, the scheme that had been simmering in my brain since I looked upward to these heights the previous morning, seemed more than ever practicable and at last found utterance: "Could we not manage to get down this way?" and the hope of crowning the triumph by a traverse of the mountain, conquering its reputed inaccessible ramparts (and that, too, in a descent), together with the prospect of an absolutely first-class climb, decided the reply in the affirmative. True, at least three great bands of rock lay there below us, any one of which might prove an insurmountable obstacle and necessitate a retracing of our footsteps, with the probable consequence of a night out, at a considerable altitude, among the icy fastnesses; but we had found *some* crack or cranny heretofore in their courses on the farther side, and—well, we would try to find an equally convenient right of way on this face, too.

So, after a halt of nearly two hours, at 1.40 we embarked upon our final essay.

Well roped and moving generally one at a time, we clambered downward foot by foot, now balancing upon the narrow ridge, 5000 feet of space at our right hand; then scrambling down a broken wall-end, the rocks so friable that hand-hold after hand-hold had to be abandoned, and often half a dozen tested before a safe one could be found; now, when the ridge became too jagged or too sheer, making our cautious way along a tiny ledge or down the face itself, clinging to the cold buttresses, our fingers tightly clutching the scant projection of some icy knob, or digging into small interstices between the rocks; anon, an ice-slope had to be negotiated with laborious cutting of steps in the hard wall-like surface; and again, cliff after cliff must be reconnoitred, its slippery upper rim traversed until a cleft was found and a gymnastic descent effected to the ice-bound declivity that fell away beneath its base.

For close upon 2000 feet the utmost skill and care were imperative at every step; for scarcely half a dozen could be taken in that distance where an unroped man who slipped would not inevitably have followed the rejected hand-holds and *débris*, that hurtled down in leaps and bounds to crash in fragments on the rocks and boulders far below.

But with a rope a careful party of experienced mountaineers is absolutely free from danger; and, though it took our usually rapid trio three and a half hours to descend some 1800 feet, our confidence was fully vindicated, for nothing insurmountable obstructed our advance, and, after a brief halt below the last cliff wall (where sundry relics of the Walling expedition were observed), a gay descent, on snow that needed no step-cutting, brought us soon after six o'clock to easier, continuous rocks, where we unroped.

A speedy spell swinging down rocks, with an occasional glissade, landed us on the glacier in forty minutes, and an hour later, in the gathering darkness, we approached the camp, after an absence of thirteen hours and a half, greeted by shouts of welcome and congratulation from Peyto and Sinclair (who had seen us on the summit) and strains of martial music from the latter's violin.

Before turning in, we took a last look at the splendid obelisk above us, radiant in the moonlight against the dark star-strewn canopy of heaven. A last look it proved; for next morning we awoke to a white world, with nothing visible of Mt. Assiniboine but an occasional glimpse, through sweeping, leaden clouds, of its steep flanks deeply covered with the freshly fallen snow.

The return journey was begun at one o'clock that afternoon, and Desolation Valley was traversed in the snow and rain, our chill encampment being made in the flat pasture at the head of Simpson Valley.

Next day we made a most tremendous march in the teeth of a driving snow-storm. The valley, with its gaunt, spectral tree-trunks, was drearier and more weird than ever; the blackened timber, outlined against the dazzling snow, showed in a mazy network; the bushes, with their load of fruit, peeped out forlornly, amid their wintry environment, and every flower bore a tiny burden on its drooping head. The steep ascent of 1500 feet was made in ever deepening snow, and on the alp above we met the fierce blasts of the keen north wind, sweeping across the unprotected uplands. Wearied with our forced marches and two long days of arduous climbing, the tramping through soft, drifting snow, the steady upward trend of our advance and the hard conflict with the driving storm, it was with deep relief that we crossed the final ridge and could descend to calmer regions through the dark, snow-laden pines. Still on we went, down Healy Creek to the Bow Valley, where the packers camped with their tired horses, and the guides and I tramped on two hours more to Banff, arriving there just five days and five hours from the time of our departure.

Our toils were over. In spite of adverse weather conditions, the expedition had been intensely interesting from start to finish, and more than a success from a climber's point of view; and the fact that the ascent was made upon the last possible day the weather would permit that season gave a dramatic touch that added an extra spice of satisfaction to the accomplishment of a mountaineering feat, perhaps the most sensational then achieved in North America.

[1] "The Rockies of Canada," p. 89.
[2] W. D. Wilcox in "The Rockies of Canada," p. 109.

Victory at Last: The First
Ascent of Huascarán

ANNIE S. PECK

On Monday after an early breakfast of soup, improving in this way our last opportunity for a wood fire, at the early hour of 7:15 we entered upon the glacier, the four Indians all wearing climbing irons, as enough had been made so that each of us had a pair. The Swiss guides, however, preferred to dispense with them, and I as well, unless they should prove absolutely necessary, for after my return to Yungay, I had discovered that two toes and the whole top of my right foot had been frost-bitten, on account of one strap, which was a little short, having been drawn so tight as to impede the circulation in that foot. Gabriel also had had two of his toes frost-bitten, but not severely.

During Saturday forenoon the clouds had left the mountain so that, with two days of sunshine on the fresh snow and the nightly freezing, we found the glacier in better condition than ever before. Going straight up from our more favourable starting point, in two hours we arrived at the site of our previous first camp. After a brief halt we pushed on to our second camp, where we had luncheon. Under the excellent conditions, with four good porters, and no double work, we continued in the afternoon almost up to the site of our fourth camp. Pausing about four o'clock, well pleased with our day's work, we pitched our tent in a sheltered spot, well up in the saddle, at the foot of a more than vertically inclined snow wall.

In spite of our favourable position, the night was windy and the morning cold, but soon after eight we were on our way. Having safely negotiated the steep ascent concluded by the perpendicular bit of blue ice (which we reached by going up in zigzags farther to the right, then walking along the ledge to the place where Gabriel is cutting steps), we were soon near the foot of the great wall, in the midst of seracs, crevasses, caverns, and every variety of difficulties. The way we had previously taken was blocked by the disappearance of a snow bridge, but Gabriel found another route, threading his way among hollows and immense crevasses till we came to the more solid part of the wall with an angle of approximately 80° or 85°. We went up in two divisions, as we had been climbing previously, Gabriel leading one and Rudolf the other. Thankful was I to reach the top in safety and throw myself down for rest and luncheon, knowing that the remainder of the way to the top of the saddle was comparatively easy.

Yet in this easy part we had an adventure, which was the more surprising. A crevasse extending nearly all the way across the saddle was spanned by a bridge of so doubtful appearance that Rudolf who was leading went over on hands and knees. I, being in the middle of the rope and also much lighter, walked carefully across, while Rudolf was sitting on the farther slope with the rope around his ice axe. Taking a position above him in the same manner, I re-enforced his strength with mine; Lucas at the end of the rope then followed, walking, as on account of his pack it would have been impossible for him to crawl.

Suddenly there was a cry. Lucas had disappeared. Of course the alpen rope was strong and our hold was good. Rudolf admitted later that my help was of real value. My wrists, it happens, are disproportionately strong. Lucas, though uncomfortable, was probably in no danger. Gabriel at the head of the second rope, exhorted the other three men to untie quickly, this more by motion than by speech, for neither of the Swiss had picked up much Spanish; he then threw down one end of the rope to Lucas, who, luckily, was the most intelligent of the Indians, and preserved his coolness. Though he had fallen head down, as is usual, he was able to right himself and tie this rope to the one about his waist. Then the men below and Rudolf and I above pulled him up to the surface, when he got out on the lower side, naturally without his pack, which, with many other articles, again contained the stove. As without this further advance was impossible, when the men had made the crossing at a point farther north, and Lucas had declined the honour, Gabriel undertook its recovery. The crevasse luckily was neither very wide nor deep, so Gabriel, at the end of the rope which was held carefully by the others, climbed down where they had crossed to a depth of thirty feet, walked along the bottom to the broken bridge, and after some minutes of suspense appeared again with the rescued baggage. Such an effort at this altitude, over 19,000 feet, was doubly severe, and Gabriel paused a few moments, leaning over with his head on his ice axe, before he was able to proceed. I, meanwhile, remaining where Rudolf and I had crossed, had improved my time by taking photographs of the crevasse. Afterwards, at the top of the very last wall, Adrian stumbled and almost fell backwards, dropping his alpenstock, which happily lodged not far down and was recovered again by Gabriel.

In fairly good season we encamped that night on the plain at the top of the saddle, in two days from the snow line, a feat which I had previously hoped with Swiss guides to be able to accomplish. The exceptionally cold day, the coldest I had experienced in my six efforts on this mountain, was followed by a high wind at night—an unpleasant contrast to our previous experience here, when all three nights had been almost windless. In the early morning, I thought it wiser to postpone our final effort till the fierce wind should abate; we should also be in better condition following a rest from two long and hard days' labour. Had I expected to make the attempt on this day I should have insisted upon an earlier start. Both guides, however, though not anxious to set out early, were in favour of going, asserting that we might find less wind higher up, if not that we could turn back. On the contrary, unless the wind died down altogether, it was more likely to be worse above, and it was against my better judgment that I yielded to their wishes.

At the late hour, for such a climb, of eight o'clock, we set forth, myself and the two guides only, as with the two Swiss the Indians would not add to the safety of the party, probably the reverse. For the cold ascent, I was wearing every stitch of clothing that I had brought: three suits of light weight woollen underwear, two pairs of tights, canvas knickerbockers, two flannel waists, a little cardigan jacket, two sweaters, and four pairs of woollen stockings; but as most of the clothing was porous it was inadequate to keep out the wind, for which I had relied upon the eskimo suit now at the bottom of a crevasse. I had not really needed it before, nor worn it except at night. Now when I wanted it badly, it was gone. I am often asked if my progress is not impeded by the weight of so much clothing, to which I answer, No. All of the articles were light, and garments which cling closely to the body are not burdensome. I never noticed the weight at all. A skirt, on the contrary, however short and light, anything depending from the waist or shoulders, is some hindrance to movement and of noticeable weight. I had not an ounce of strength to spare for superfluities, neither do I consider that an abbreviated skirt would add to the gracefulness of my appearance, or if it did, that this, upon the mountain, would be of the slightest consequence: while in rock climbing the shortest skirt may be an added source of danger.

A woollen face and head mask, which I had purchased in La Paz, provided with a good nose piece as well as eye-holes, mouth-slit, and a rather superfluous painted moustache, protected my head, face, and neck from the wind. An extra one, which I had brought along, a rather better article except that it left the nose exposed, I offered to Gabriel, Rudolf having brought a hood of his own. Somewhat to my surprise, as the guides had seemed always to despise the cold and to regard my warnings as superfluous, this offer was accepted with alacrity. My hands were covered with a pair of vicuña mittens made for me in La Paz with two thicknesses of fur, one turned outside and one in. For these, until the day before, I had had no use; they now kept even my cold hands comfortable. In fact, as the sun rose higher, they became too warm and were exchanged for two pairs of wool mittens, one of which, however, did not cover the fingers. The fur mittens, being too large to go into my pocket or leather bag, were handed over to Rudolf, who was next to me, to put into his rück-sack.

I had repeatedly warned the men of the great danger of freezing above, not so much from the actual cold as from the rarity of the air, telling them how Pelissier (one of Conway's guides), with two pairs of stockings, had had his feet frozen on Aconcagua so that they turned black, and he barely escaped losing them; how Zurbriggan, Maquignaz, and others had been frost-bitten on Aconcagua and Sorata. In spite of this, they hardly seemed to realise the necessity of so much care. They stated that their shoes would admit of but one pair of their heavy woollen stockings and seemed quite unconcerned as to the possibilities of freezing.

The men carried food and tea for luncheon (the latter I had sat up to make the night before, after the rest had gone to bed), the hypsometer to take observations, and my camera. The mercurial barometer I had left in Yungay, from misgivings that I might have to carry it if it was brought along. As there was no extra clothing of mine to transport, since I had put it all on, I ventured to ask if one of the guides could carry up the warm poncho, fearing that I might need it when we paused for luncheon or on the summit. It was rather heavy and a considerable burden at that altitude, but Gabriel said he could take it; to the fact of my extreme, apparently superfluous caution, and of Gabriel's willingness and strength, I certainly owe the possession and soundness of all my limbs, as I also owe Gabriel my life. The canteen of alcohol, which was used to light the fire of our kerosene stove, and from which also a small draught night and morning was given to the Indians, was carried some distance from the tent lest the temptation to drink this in our long absence should prove too much for them. When the can was deposited in the snow, with which it was half covered to make sure that it would not blow away, I inquired, "Are you sure you can find this on our return?" Both men replied that they certainly could.

Considering the altitude our progress seemed rapid. On the slope above the camp no steps were needed, but when, after an hour or less, we turned to the left, making a long traverse among great crevasses, walls, and appalling downward slopes, it was necessary that steps should be cut all of the time. The snow was in a worse condition than before. It had been hard enough then (though softer in the middle of the day), but not so smooth. Now the severe cold had made it harder still, while the high wind had blown from the exposed slopes all of the lighter particles, leaving a surface smooth as glass, such as Gabriel said he had never seen in Switzerland except in small patches.

Coming out at length upon a ridge where we were more exposed to the wind I felt the need of my vicuña mittens which had seemed too warm below. I delayed asking for a while, hoping to come to a better standing place; but as none appeared, calling a halt I approached Rudolf, who continually held the rope for me, while Gabriel was cutting the steps, so that the delays necessary on the previous ascent were avoided. Rudolf, taking the mittens from his rücksack with some black woven sleeves I had earlier worn on my forearms, tucked the former under one arm saying, "Which will you have first?" I had it on the end of my tongue to exclaim, " Look out you don't lose my mittens!" But like most men, the guides were rather impatient of what they considered unnecessary advice or suggestions from a woman, even an employer; so, thinking, he surely will be careful of my mittens, I refrained and said, "Give me the armlets!" A second later Rudolf cried, "I have lost one of your mittens!" I did not see it go, it slipped out at the back, but anything dropped on that smooth slope, even without the high wind, might as well have gone over a precipice.

I was angry and alarmed at his inexcusable carelessness, but it was useless to talk. I could do that after we got down, though under subsequent circumstances I never did. I hastily put my two brown woollen mittens and one red mitt on my left hand, the vicuña fur on my right which generally held the ice axe and was therefore more exposed. Onward and upward for hours we pressed, when at length we paused for luncheon being too cold and tired to eat the meat which had frozen in the rück-sack, and the almost equally hard bread; though we ate Peter's chocolate and raisins, of which we had taken an occasional nibble, each from his own pocket, all along the way. (I had found a few raisins in one of the stores and bought all they had.) The tea, too, was partially frozen in Rudolf's canteen. About two o'clock, Taugwalder declared himself unable to proceed. I was for leaving him there and going on with Gabriel, but the latter urged him onward, suggesting that by leaving his rück-sack, he might be able to continue with us. This, after a short rest, he did, finding that we were going on anyway. Gabriel now carried the camera and hypsometer, in addition to the poncho, besides cutting the steps.

The latter part of the climb was especially steep. All, suffering from cold and fatigue, required frequent brief halts, though we sat down but twice on the way up and not at all at the top. At last we were approaching our goal. Rounding the apparent summit we found a broad way of the slightest grade leading gently to the northern end of the ridge, though from below, the highest point had appeared to be at the south. On the ridge, the wind was stronger than ever, and I suddenly realised that my left hand was insensible and freezing. Twitching off my mittens, I found that the hand was nearly black. Rubbing it vigorously with snow, I soon had it aching badly, which signified its restoration; but it would surely freeze again (it was now three o'clock) in the colder hours of the late afternoon and night. My over-caution in having the poncho brought up now proved my salvation. This heavy shawl or blanket, with a slit in the middle, slipped over my head, kept me fairly warm to the end, protecting my hand somewhat, as well as my whole body. At the same time, it was awkward to wear, reaching nearly to my knees, and was the cause of my slipping and almost of my death on the way down. But for the loss of my fur mitten I should not have been compelled to wear it except, as intended, on the summit.

A little farther on, Gabriel suggested our halting for the observations, as the wind might be worse at the extremity of the ridge. The slope, however, was so slight that there was probably no difference. Rudolf now untied and disappeared. I was so busy over the hypsometer that I did not notice where he went, realising only that he was not there. While, careful not to expose too much my left hand, I shielded the hypsometer from the wind as well as I was able with the poncho, Gabriel struck match after match in vain. Once he lighted the candle, but immediately it went out. After striking twenty matches, Gabriel said, "It is useless; we must give it up." With Rudolf's assistance in holding the poncho we might have done better. But it was past three. That dread descent was before us. Sadly I packed away the instrument, believing it better to return alive, if possible, than to risk further delay. It was a great disappointment not to make the expected contribution to science; perhaps to have broken the world's record, without being able to prove it; but to return alive seemed still more desirable, even though in ignorance of the exact height to which we had attained.

Rudolf now appeared and informed me that *he* had been on to the summit, instead of remaining to assist with the hypsometer. I *was* enraged. I had told them, long before, that, as it was my expedition, I should like, as is customary, to be the first one to place my foot at the top, even though I reached it through their instrumentality. It would not lessen their honour and I was paying the bills. I had related how a few feet below the top of Mt. St. Elias, Maquignaz had stepped back and said to the Duke of the Abruzzi, "Monsieur, à vous la glorie!" And Rudolf, who with little grit had on the first attempt turned back at 16,000 feet, compelling me to make this weary climb over again, who this time had not done half so much work as Gabriel, who had wished to give up an hour below the summit, instead of remaining here with us to render assistance with the observations, had coolly walked on to the highest point! I had not *dreamed* of such an act. The disappointment may have been trivial. Of course it made no real difference to the honour to which I was entitled, but of a certain personal satisfaction, long looked forward to, I had been robbed. Once more I resolved, if ever we got down again, to give that man a piece of my mind, a large one; but after all I never did, for then he had troubles enough of his own, and words would not change the fact. Now, without a word, I went on.

Though the grade was slight, I was obliged to pause several times in the fierce wind, once leaning my head on my ice axe for a few seconds before I could continue to the goal. Gabriel stopped a short distance from the end, advising me not to go too near the edge, which I had no inclination to do, passing but a few feet beyond him. I should like to have looked down into the Llanganuco Gorge, whence I had looked up at the cliff and the thick overhanging cornice, such as impended above the east and west cliffs also. We had, therefore, kept in the centre of the broad ridge, at least 40 feet wide, it may have been more: it seemed wider than an ordinary city street. Had it been earlier in the day, being particularly fond of precipices, and this would have been the biggest I had ever looked down, I should have ventured near the north edge with Gabriel holding the rope; but now I did not care to hazard delay from the possibility of breaking through the cornice.

My first thought on reaching the goal was, "I am here at last, after all these years; but shall we ever get down again?" I said nothing except, "Give me the camera," and as rapidly as possible took views towards the four quarters of the heavens, one including Gabriel. The click of the camera did not sound just right, and fearing that I was getting no pictures at all, I did not bother to have Gabriel try to take a photograph of me. This I afterwards regretted, as I should like to have preserved such a picture for my own pleasure. But in later days I was thankful indeed that in spite of high wind and blowing snow the other pictures did come out fairly; for it is pictures *from* the summit that tell the tale, and not the picture of someone standing on a bit of rock or snow which may be anywhere.

The view was nothing unless I could have gone to the edge of the broad surface. The other twin peak at the south, obviously a little higher, as I had always maintained, shut out the rest of the range in that direction, and we were so much above the mountains at the north that not going quite to the end, I did not see even Huandoy on the other side of the Gorge. The Cordillera Negra I had long been familiar with from the valley below and all the way up, while the view of the snow mountains towards the east, which I particularly desired to see, was cut off by our distance from the edge, save at the southeast where some peaks far below were visible.

There was no pleasure here, hardly a feeling of triumph, in view of my disappointment over the
observations, and my dread of the long and terrible
descent. If ever I were safely down, there would be
plenty of time to rejoice. It was half past three, and
soon would be dark. Seven hours coming up! Would
it take us as long to return? Steep rocks and icy
slopes are far more dangerous to descend, and especially perilous after dark; with those small steps, the
prospect was indeed terrifying: so without a
moment's rest we began our retreat. The summit
ridge, at least a quarter of a mile in length, was
quickly traversed, at that altitude a slight change in
grade making as much difference as in bicycling.

Gabriel had led nearly all the way up, cutting
most, if not all, of the steps. Rudolf had been second, in order to hold the rope for me, avoiding all
possible delay. Going down I was roped in the middle, the more usual position for the amateur, Rudolf
at first taking the lead and Gabriel occupying the
more responsible place in the rear; for in descending,
the rear is the post of honour, as that of leader in the
ascent; since the strongest of a party must be above,
holding the rope in case of a slip on the part of the
amateur in front. A guide, of course, is never
expected to slip and a good one practically never
does. If the rear guard goes, as a rule all are lost.

The guides' shoes being well studded with nails
they had not cared to wear the climbing irons, to

which they were unaccustomed, and which by impeding the circulation would have made their feet colder. My shoes were more poorly provided, as it was impossible to procure in New York such nails as are employed in the Alps. I had intended to wear the crampons which would have made them unnecessary, but on Gabriel's advice had left them below, lest my feet should be frozen, as the one previously touched by the frost would have greater liability.

At the end of the ridge difficulties began. A smooth slope of 60° is never pleasant. From the beginning of the descent I greatly feared the outcome, but we had to go down and the faster we could go, yet carefully, the better. Presently I saw something black fly away: one of Rudolf's mittens. One might suppose that after losing mine he would have been the more careful of his own. When I inquired afterwards how he came to lose it, he said he laid it down on that icy slope to fasten his shoe. Of course the wind blew it away. Later I learned that after dark he lost the second mitten. This he said was in trying to change from one hand to the other. He thought he had hold of it, but his hand being numb, he could not feel it, and this went also. If he had spoken we should have halted, so that he could make sure. His carelessness seems incredible and inexcusable, and brought disastrous consequences to himself and nearly to us all, almost costing our lives. Probably I should not have slipped, had I not been obliged on account of the loss of my fur mittens to wear the poncho which occasionally prevented my seeing the steps. Certainly Rudolf himself would not have slipped any more than Gabriel, if his hands had not been frozen and himself chilled through, so that one foot froze also; thus his footing was insecure and his grip on his ice axe less firm. It seems almost a miracle that he slipped only once and that we at last got down alive. His carelessness may perhaps be explained by the fact of his being so much affected by the altitude that it rendered him stupid, as below he had seemed as thoughtful and as careful as Gabriel. The latter, however, I had regarded as a trifle the more intelligent, as he was evidently the stronger.

On this steep slope, I deeply regretted the absence of my climbing irons, for the steps were small indeed. On the Jungfrau those made by my guide Baumann were very large, requiring from ten to twenty blows; but this would never do on the much longer slope of Huascarán. Two or three hacks for each were all that Gabriel could give, so they were not half as large as his shoes, little more than toe-holes. They did well enough going up but not on the way down. While zigzagging I missed a step, sat down and slid a few feet, but Gabriel above was holding the rope tight and I easily regained my footing.

Some time after dark it seemed advisable for Gabriel to take the lead (such matters of course I left to them), perhaps because he was more familiar with the way or could see better on the long sloping traverse across the wide face of the mountain in the midst of caverns, crevasses, and those dreadful slopes and precipices; yet as a slide anywhere would have been fatal, one place was just as bad as another, except as some parts were steeper. Gabriel estimated the incline as from 40° to 60° through the greater part of the distance. I had brought with me a clinometer, but never had time and strength to use it. I had been on measured slopes of 42° and 53° on my first mountain, and judging from these, had never afterwards over-estimated any that had been capable of verification. My opinion here coincides with Gabriel's. If anyone should not accept it, the matter is of little consequence as compared with the altitude, which unfortunately I had been obliged to leave unmeasured. But that could be determined at a later date. Whatever it might be, the *fact* of my ascent would stand.

My recollection of the descent is as of a horrible nightmare, though such I never experienced. The little moon seemed always at my back, casting a shadow over the place where I must step. The poncho would sway in the wind, and, with my motion as I was in the act of stepping, would sometimes conceal the spot where my foot should be placed. Although my eye for distance is good, my foot once missed the step, slipping then on the smooth slope so that I fell, as usual in a sitting posture, crying out at the same time to warn the guides. I expected nothing serious, but to my horror, I did not remain where I was. Still sitting I began to slide down that glassy, ghastly incline. As we were all nearly in the same line, I slid at least fifteen feet before coming to a halt, when checked by the rope. Now to get back! The guides called to me to get up, but being all in a heap, with the rope tight around my waist, I was unable to move. The guides therefore came together just above and hauled me up the slope. Thankful again to be in the line of the steps, though more alarmed than ever, I went onward, resolved to be more careful. But again I slipped, and again slid far below. While from the beginning of the descent, I had greatly feared the outcome, after these slips my terror increased. Several times I declared that we should never get down alive. I begged Gabriel to stop for the night and make a cave in the snow, but, saying this was impossible, he continued without a pause. The snow indeed was too hard, yet in some cavern or crevasse I thought we could find shelter from the wind. Gabriel afterwards asserted that if we had stopped we should all have frozen to death.

Again and again I slipped, five or six times altogether, but always Gabriel held his ground firmly. Always, too, I clung to my ice axe; so to his shout, "Have you your axe?" I could respond in the affirmative, and sometimes with it could help myself back again. Once when I had slipped, I was astonished to see Rudolf dart by me, wondering how he could help me by running far below. Afterwards I learned, that with my pull he, too, had slipped and Gabriel's strong arm alone saved us all from destruction. Had he given way, after sliding some distance we should all have dropped off thousands of feet below. When he saw Rudolf go, Gabriel thought for a moment that we were all lost; but his axe was well placed with the rope around it, and although two fingers were caught between the rope and the ice axe, knowing it was life or death he stood firm until Rudolf recovered himself. Otherwise, Gabriel said afterwards, he never despaired but thought only of going on. Rudolf, however, to my great astonishment, for I had supposed I was the only one who was frightened, confessed later that he never expected to get down alive.

The cold and fatigue, the darkness and shadow, the poncho blowing before me, the absence of climbing irons, the small steps, the steep glassy slopes, presented an extraordinary combination of difficulties. It seemed that the way would never end. I tried to comfort myself with the reflection that accidents do not run in our family, that nothing serious, more than broken ribs or knee-pan—these not in climbing—ever *had* happened to me; but also I was aware that people do not generally die but once. I said to myself, for the first time in my life, I *must* keep cool and do my best, and so I did; but after several of those horrible slides—Well, there was nothing to do but to plod along.

At last, at last—! Before I was aware that we had emerged from among those terrible abysses to the slope above the tent, Gabriel said "Now we are safe; and if you like you can slide." What a tremendous relief! I sat down happily, Gabriel walking ahead and guiding me with the rope. At first it was fun, then I went too fast, bobbing here and there, bumping, floundering, finally turning around, sliding on my back, and giving my head a hard whack before I came to a halt. However, we were nearly down and walked on to the tent where we arrived at half past ten, thankful for rest and shelter. There was nothing to drink, we were too tired to eat or sleep, but glad indeed to sit down in safety, too fatigued at first even to lie down.

Poor Rudolf! His hands were badly frozen, his fingers black, the left hand worse than the right. He was rubbing them weakly with snow, first one, then the other. I told him he should rub them harder to get up circulation; I felt I ought to do it myself, but somehow sat there and did not. Gabriel did not offer to, either. He no doubt was thoroughly worn out, too. One of the Indians might have done it, but after greeting us, they huddled up on their own side of the tent and went to sleep again, and no one asked them. There was not room in the tent for seven persons to lie down, so we three had one side of the pole, the four Indians the other. They curled up in their ponchos, two with heads one side and two the other, half sitting, with feet toward the middle. I was unable to use my sleeping bag properly on this trip, for there would have been no room left for the guides. I had therefore taken the blankets from the canvas cover and spread them out with other blankets brought from the Vinatéas, and we had managed to be fairly comfortable. Heretofore I had taken the inside as being warmer, but to-night after sitting awhile, I took the outside, leaving the place in the centre for Rudolf.

The wind continued to blow hard all night and the next day. We did not rise early and no one proposed descending, though I felt that Rudolf ought to get down as soon as possible. Gabriel went up for the can of alcohol, looking at the same time for a leather bag which had been attached to my belt and which had disappeared, doubtless in one of those terrible earlier slides, rather than on the last, since it was nowhere to be found. Also, as I had feared, the can of alcohol did not appear; whether covered by blowing snow or whether the Indians had gone up and drunk it, then concealing the can (though of this they gave no sign), or what became of it we could not tell. Being without fire we had no water, soup, or tea. I tried for an hour or more by burning matches to heat and ignite some oil in the place where the alcohol should have gone. Once I had it burning for a moment, but after using a whole box of matches, I gave it up. Quinua meal with snow and sugar, or the last two alone were our best substitutes for water.

Friday we were somewhat rested, the wind abated, and we started down. Soon we came to another icy slope, not very steep, where the Indians with their climbing irons passed easily, but where I began to slide standing. Gabriel appeared rather vexed with me, but I did not see how I could help it. The guides weighed much more than I, and with the heavy nails on their boots doubtless made indentations which I could not do. However, by going slowly, with care and with the aid of the rope, I passed the glassy surface safely.

At the top of the great wall, I decided to put on my crampons, preferring on the whole to risk freezing my toes rather than losing my life. Gabriel had proposed that all descend together. I said "No, one at a time, if it does take longer." I had climbed my mountain at last and did not wish to be killed on the way down. Our three ropes being tied together, the others descended one by one, Rudolf first, then the Indians, while Gabriel, aided by Lucas, lowered the rope from above and then hauled it up for the next man. The rope reached but part way down to a convenient ledge of snow, where the men waited in the midst of crevasses until all had come down. Gabriel had estimated the entire wall at 300 feet.

After my return to Yungay, I took the trouble to measure the ropes; the total being 180 feet, it seemed that his judgment was fairly accurate. I should not have ventured a guess myself, not being used to making estimates of that nature. While descending this upper part of the wall, one of the Indians slipped, falling, he said, *dos cuadras*—two blocks—an evident exaggeration, as the rope was held above; but it was fortunate we were not together, or his slip might have proved fatal to all.

I was the last to go down except Gabriel and Lucas. For a time all was well. Of course we went backwards as on a ladder. Then for some reason I moved a little more slowly, while the men seemed to lower the rope more rapidly. I did not like to proceed with the rope so loose; as there was a deep crevasse in the wall close by, the upper outside edge of which gave a seat, with a resting place for one foot below, I sat down there, hoping that the men might perceive that the rope was not taut and draw it part way up again. As they did not, I untied and threw it off, shouting to them to pull it up. Evidently they could not hear and continued to lower it farther, the end going down into the crevasse behind me. At last they pulled it up and there I sat perched half way on the wall, unable to see the men above or those below, and obliged to remain motionless on my icy seat, where a fall backwards would precipitate me into a black and profound abyss, and a slip forward to a greater depth down the face of the wall into some immense cavern or *bergschrund* at the bottom. So long as I sat still, I was safe, though when at last Lucas came down, I had to crowd myself into the smallest possible space in order to give him room to pass by. Gabriel came last; he did not need anyone to hold the rope for him. I was glad to see him, though I expected a scolding for having untied and being left here halfway; but he was unexpectedly amiable, and tying me to the rope of which he had kept the upper end, I went down without any trouble till we came to the men below. Such an array of *bergschründe* and caverns, a perfect medley of enormous hollows, great snow masses, and precipices, I never elsewhere witnessed: a wonderful sight which would delight the heart of any mountaineer. From here we went on together. It would seem that in this section at some time there must be tremendous snow falls, great masses splitting off from the side slopes above; but at this season there was no sign of snow avalanches, except as overhanging ice walls and immense irregular masses below, gave evidence that at some seasons great operations were here conducted. The wall was not of hard ice but of solid snow or nêvé, the space between the two peaks being filled in with snow, obviously hundreds of feet deep. Here in the middle of the saddle, a rock wall beneath has evidently caused a tremendous mass of snow to break off nearly all the way across, leaving a snow wall the solid part of which was about the length of our united ropes, 180 feet, with 100 feet more of irregular cavernous and crevassed descent. The solid part in places lacked little of the perpendicular, equalling the angle of the cliff on the Fünf-fingerspitze above the Daumen-scharte.

After descending, also one at a time, the shorter ice wall farther down, we could go more rapidly, except for delay on a steep traverse, where first one of the *peónes*, then another, slid twenty or thirty feet. At length all dangers were over; we passed one old camp after another, eager to reach the rocks where we could have fire and water, of which we had been destitute for more than forty-eight hours.

At the edge of the glacier, before sunset, the men paused where a few streams trickled, and drank and drank, while I sat patiently waiting till they had their fill and one of them was ready to bring a bucket of water from a larger stream at a distance. Within the next five minutes, I drank four tin cupfuls, a greater quantity at once than ever before in my life. Presently we had soup and tea. It was a quiet moonlight evening and with the Indians preferring to sleep outside the tent, we should have been very comfortable and happy had it not been for Rudolf's frozen hands and foot. He dared not take off one boot lest he should be unable to put it on again in the morning.

Soon after sunrise on Saturday we started down, as I was anxious to get Rudolf to Yungay and a physician. This time, descending by the proper route, we arrived about ten o'clock at the mine, where we found Señor Jaramillo with the horses, this being the appointed day. After breakfast we hastened on to Yungay, I at least rejoicing that I should not have to come that way again; though the sad condition of Rudolf, then and always, greatly marred the satisfaction of my triumph. His misfortune seemed indeed to outweigh any benefit derived from the ascent, my only consolation being that it was his own fault and not a necessary consequence of the climb, as the soundness of myself and Gabriel proved. I learned afterwards that Rudolf, in spite of all I had said about the cold, had even left an extra flannel shirt in the tent at the saddle while he went to the top. This, by keeping his body warmer, might have slightly lessened his calamity. Also there were four pairs of mittens in the tent, some of which might have been carried, if one had supposed that any would be lost.

As I rode along the valley and looked up at that great magnificent mountain conquered at last, after so many years of struggle, days and weeks of hardship, and now at such cost, I felt almost like shaking my fist at it and saying, "I have beaten you at last and I shall never have to go up there again," but I didn't.

The Ascent of Mount Cook

FREDA DU FAUR

We set off on the evening of November 30th, accompanied by Miss Murray Aynsley, who wished to come with us as far as the Hooker hut. After crossing the river, we wandered through grassy meadows filled with spring flowers, mostly white, as nearly all the New Zealand mountain flowers are. The path rising gently upward brought us in about three miles to the terminal Hooker moraine, over which we had to clamber—pathless, of course; we then descended again and crossed a rushing mountain torrent, over slippery boulders. This often means wet feet and an involuntary bath for the timid or careless. On this occasion we arrived quite safely at the other side, and began to struggle up the steep and stony path, which rises about a thousand feet in the three miles between here and the hut. Graham and a pack-horse joined us about an hour later; and just as we were preparing our evening meal, a distant hail from the regions of the Copland Pass announced that Alex was over from Westland. Soon we distinguished him scrambling down the rocks, and we were shortly all shaking hands and asking a dozen different questions that no one had time to answer. He had made a record trip, coming through in one day instead of two, being anxious not to lose any of the good weather. We were soon deep in plans and discussing our chances of a successful ascent with that rabid enthusiasm that distinguishes the sportsman of all varieties, and is usually so very boring and unintelligible to the outsider. Calming down a little, we had our supper outside on the grass; and after it was finished, wrapped ourselves in rugs, and sprawled in various graceful attitudes in the grass, watching the afterglow creep up peak after peak, till it lit the topmost crest of Mount Cook with one triumphant wave of scarlet, which overflowing, spilled down its flanks in runnels of fire, lingering longest in some rocky cavern, where it glowed orange, crimson, and red, till the very heart of the mountain seemed aglow. Shortly after sunset a bitter wind sprang up, and we were glad to retire to the shelter of our hut and very soon to bed, as we proposed an early start next morning. Alas for our hopes, by midnight the hut was creaking and groaning like a ship in a heavy sea, and straining at the wire cables that bind it to the ground, under the onslaught of a fierce westerly gale. Sleep was impossible; it seemed as if each moment we would be lifted bodily and blown over the edge of the moraine, on whose side the hut is perched, and deposited in the glacier 200 feet below. At dawn the gale showed no signs of moderating, so though the day was perfectly fine, we had to give up all idea of starting and spend the day in and about the hut. The enforced rest really did us more good than harm; but at the time, impatient as we were to get away, we did not look upon it in the light of a blessing. The following morning, December 2nd, all was calm again, and we set off at 5.15 a.m. Both the Grahams were heavily laden with about 50-lb. swags. In vain I remonstrated; they were determined I should have every luxury as well as necessity, and they would not lighten them by so much as a pound. No woman ever had two more kind, considerate, and trusty companions. Words of mine can add but little to their reputation, for the Graham brothers are known and honoured from one end of New Zealand to the other; as guides, mountaineers, and men, their country is justly proud of them. But I would like to take this opportunity of publicly expressing my appreciation of all they so willingly and cheerfully have done for me; quite simply, and as a matter of course, in a spirit of pure-minded chivalry that would not have shamed a member of King Arthur's "table round."

Everything went well with us this glorious summer morning. Fresh from our enforced rest, we made excellent time over the tedious miles of moraine, and soon descended on to the clear ice of the Hooker. At the icefall we had but little difficulty, as the crevasses were only just opening out; not having to leave the glacier for the rocks saved us hours of work. The whole expedition to the bivouac was child's play compared to our former journey, and we shortened the time by three hours, arriving at 11 a.m. As on the former occasion, it was unbearably hot, and by one o'clock we were enveloped in a thick south fog. As this is an excellent weather sign in New Zealand, no one was at all disturbed.

After fixing up the bivouac and having an hour's rest, the guides set off to kick steps for the morning, so that we could start before dawn; returning about 5.30 p.m., they reported everything in a most satisfactory state. They had walked over the schrund at the junction of rock and snow which had blocked us the year before, and followed up a snow couloir for about 1,000 feet. These steps would save us some stiff rock-work in the morning and about an hour in point of time. Cheered by such news as this, dinner was a jubilant meal; and after it was over we crawled into our sleeping-bags as a protection against the evening chill and waited for the sunset. The fog was rapidly clearing, and as the setting sun's rays pierced through the thin mist there began a series of the most wonderful colour effects it is possible to imagine. They were beautifully soft and yet extraordinarily vivid. We saw the distant mountains through a luminous curtain of softest transparency. Away on the horizon outlined against pale green evening sky rose peak after peak vivid with an edge of purest gold; the nearer cones were touched with violet and rose, while over Baker's Saddle drifted soft little clouds of crimson and gold, which shattered themselves into rainbow mists and vanished as they touched the rugged, sun-warmed rocks that impeded their westward flight. The changes of colour were so quick it was impossible to follow them—they were here and gone in a breath. No voice was raised above a whisper; we seemed to be watching some scene in fairyland that at a sound would vanish and leave us dazed and desolated. Slowly the colours faded and the mountains were blotted out by the shadowy twilight, and innumerable stars glinted from the deep blue sky. The pageant was over, the day was done, and we who had witnessed it crept quietly to sleep, awed by a beauty such as one sees but once in a lifetime.

The evening turned exceedingly cold, and I decided that having already walked over most of the conventions since I began mountaineering, one more would matter nothing; so I suggested to the guides that they abandon their tent and save me from shivering in icy aloofness till morning. The plan worked well, and I really got some sleep, especially in the early morning when Alex lit the two "cookers" inside the tent, and a delicious sense of warmth and luxury, pervaded by a smell of methylated spirit, stole over me. The next thing I knew was a polite request to wake up and eat breakfast at 1 a.m. By 2.45 we were off; it was bright starlight, perfectly calm, and very cold. We put on the rope, lit two lanterns, and started away, Peter leading, I in the middle, and Alex bringing up the rear. The lanterns cast just enough light to show the previous night's steps. The snow was frozen and very hard and in the dim light seemed to slope away to fathomless depths. We walked along in silence for about ten minutes then suddenly something shot past me down the slope, and an expression of annoyance followed it. Peter's candle had escaped; luckily it brought up on the edge of a crevasse, and Alex was able to rescue it, while we waited and shivered. The air was so keen that every breath I drew cut me like a knife; but after about half an hour I warmed up and ceased to feel it. We crossed over the schrund and started up a steep couloir. About half way up we were able to put out the lanterns, and by the time we gained the rocks at 4 a.m. it was dawn. Our climb was up the western buttress directly under the high peak, where not a ray of sunlight could reach us. There was no temptation to linger: movement was the only chance of warmth. The rocks were good, and I began to enjoy myself immensely. Alex, who had never climbed with me before, smiled approval as I shinned my way up, disdaining his proffered assistance. So Peter told him a little story between breaths, and advised him to leave me alone unless I asked for help or he, too, might "catch it hot." At 5.30 a.m. we stopped and had hot tea from a Thermos and some biscuits. It was too cold to be still long, and we soon set off again. The rocks we were now on were shaly and rotten, so we had to be exceedingly careful to prevent danger from falling stones. We were very thankful when we rose above them and found something solid once more. We found we were making record time and were much elated, but the last 1,000 feet gave us great trouble—the rocks were coated here and there with a thin film of green ice, like glass, making hand- and foot-holds dangerous and every care necessary. We were at about 11,000 feet, and the ice was so cold that my fingers stuck when they touched it; the feeling gave me quite a shock and was most unpleasant. The same thing happened if we touched ice with the steel of our axes. At last we saw the dead-white summit gleaming above us, while the first ray of sunshine we had seen that day glinted near by. We went for it with a will, accomplishing a particularly nasty traverse over an icy couloir. When we reached the ice-cap we found it all wind-blown into projecting wavelets of ice, under which the rope caught on every possible occasion. Peter cut steps for 200 feet straight up the summit; then we turned slightly to the left, and reached some soft snow up which we could kick our way. We were within a few feet of the top. They sent me on alone the length of the rope. I gained the summit and waited for them, feeling very little, very lonely, and much inclined to cry. They caught my hands and shook them, their eyes glowing with pleasure and pride, and with an effort I swallowed the lump in my throat and laughed instead. Then we all began talking at once; it was only 8.40 a.m., and we had beaten any previous record by two hours, and I a mere woman! I felt bewildered, and could not realize that the goal I had dreamed of and striven for for years was beneath my feet. I turned to them with a flash and asked if it were "really, truly the summit of Mount Cook," whereat they laughed very much and bade me look. Truly we were on top of the world, our little island world. Nothing impeded the eye—east, west, north, and south the country unrolled itself at our feet; range after range stretched away to the foothills in the north-east. Westward the sea gleamed in the sunshine, the waves breaking on mile after mile of silvery sand. South-ward and east rolled the plains of Canterbury and Otago. Directly beneath our feet lay the Hermitage Valley filled with morning mists to the level of about 3,000 feet, out of which rose the countless spurs of the Benohau Range, like promontories

from a sea of foam. Never was such a glorious day—
not a breath of wind stirred, warm sunshine lit up
the shining snows of countless peaks and sparkled on
rushing rivers, green valleys, and far-away blue lakes.
Human nature has but a limited capacity—this wide
world was limitless. My eyes strayed from point to
point: everything was different; old landmarks were
swept away, or unrecognizable from a new angle.
With a sigh almost of relief I turned my eyes to the
little patch of snow on which we stood.

Westward, where we had ascended, it sloped gently down, and on the east, as I craned my neck to
look over the brink, it fell in one sheer precipice for
4,000 feet, and with a gasp I sat back again; on the
south we looked down upon a snow ridge sharp as a
razor, leading to the middle peak; and beyond that
again showed the rocks of the third peak. We specu-
lated on the possibilities of a complete traverse of
the three peaks from north to south, and decided it
looked very ugly and would only be possible from
south to north, taking the razor-like ridge beneath
us on the upward grade. For the time my ambitions
were satisfied, and I disclaimed any desire to attempt
it, and turned my eyes northward. Here again the
slope was not bad, and led down to Green's Saddle,
from which a wickedly jagged rock ridge led up to
New Zealand's highest virgin peak and third highest
mountain, Mount Dampier; and on again in varied
curves to the second highest peak, Mount Tasman.

We spent two hours on the summit and took many photographs. Bitterly did I regret the fact that I was the merest amateur and knew nothing, only having owned a camera two months. No one had ever taken any successful pictures from the top of Mount Cook, and none had had such a chance as this. The guides said the gods themselves must have been on my side; they had never known such a day on Mount Cook. For the first time I could look at last year's failure with equanimity—even rejoice in the defeat, since it had given us such a perfect day for our second attempt. At 11 a.m. we began the descent, Alex leading; the thought of descending the icy rocks was rather a nightmare, but we overcame them without harm by care and patience. I was congratulating myself that all was well, quite forgetting the rotten rocks lower down. They did not let us forget them for long; even now, after two years and much experience, the thought of the four hours we spent upon them makes me feel sick and shaky. We moved one at a time, and took every possible care, but now and again someone would dislodge a stone, and it would clatter down behind, or, if small, ping past like a rifle bullet. One fairly large one caught me in the middle of the back; fortunately it had not come far or fast, but it doubled me up for the time being. We had then only been on rotten rock for two hours, and had at least another two before us. I was afraid to put one foot before the other, my knees were shaky, and my bruised back one dull ache. Half an hour later, just as I was traversing an overhanging point, the whole thing gave way beneath my feet. Instinctively I jumped back, and heard an exclamation from Peter behind me, and felt the jerk of the rope as he tightened it. I stood with my face to a cliff, and a foot of rock to spare, while the stones rattled and fell in showers down to the glacier beneath; then I crawled on to Alex, who was round the corner, and Peter followed. Probably my face was white under its sunburn—I know the guides' were; without a word we all sat down in a safe place. I saw the Grahams looking furtively at me, and knew as well as if they had spoken that they were wondering how much more I could stand. As I did not know myself, I pretended not to see their glances, and drank down some hot tea and ate a little with thankfulness. After half an hour's rest we went on again; we had passed the worst and had no further adventures, and at last arrived at the snow couloir. Once down it, Alex let out a whoop; I followed his example, and the three of us raced down the soft snow towards the bivouac, laughing and excited like so many schoolchildren. Arriving, just as I turned to go into my tent, Peter caught my hand and Alex stood beside me smiling. "Now we will congratulate you, now we are safe down and have beaten all previous records. Look!" and drawing out his watch he pointed to the time, 5.30 p.m. "By Jove! six hours up, two hours there,

six and a half down; that time will take some beating, little lady," and Alex shook my other hand vigorously. "Thanks to the two finest guides in the
mountains, it will," I answered, and I slipped past
them into my tent, and throwing myself down, proceeded to rid myself of putties and boots, preparatory to a well-earned rest. We decided that we were
all too tired to do justice to a large meal, so merely
indulged in unlimited tea and a tin of frozen
peaches, which latter will always have a kindly place
in my memory as the most luscious dish ever offered
to a hot and thirsty mountaineer.

After the meal was over I threw myself on my
sleeping-bag and was shortly lost in oblivion. Waking a couple of hours later, I found that the preparations for a feast befitting the occasion were in full
swing. When all was ready we gathered round a
bubbling cooker and did justice to savoury tomato
soup, cold meat, tinned fruit and bread and butter,
the whole washed down with freshly brewed tea.
The guides' capacity for the last-mentioned item
was somewhat astounding; it vanished by the quart
with astonishing ease and rapidity. The remnants of
the feast cleared away, we crawled into our sleeping-
bags and sought our well-earned rest. I awoke once
or twice with cramped limbs, or a sharp stone digging into my anatomy, but soon dropped off to sleep
again.

First to Climb Lizard Head

ALBERT L. ELLINGWOOD

A million years ago, in the region men were to call the Silvery San Juan, the granite foundations of the earth were riven and from the fissures bubbling lava welled forth in a mighty flood. Engulfing all things living in its destructive progress, it spread far and wide over canyon, stream and mountain, and when it had spent its force, its sluggish verge enclosed a desolate area so large the king of birds could hardly circle it from dawn to dusk.

It were vain to ask how great the multitude of monsters overwhelmed beneath the sticky mud. Only the greatest of them all, the ancient ancestor of the puny Titanosaurs of a much later age, left even a trace behind. Isolated on an outstanding ridge and slowly swallowed up in the inexorable ooze, he struggled despairingly, even when altogether submerged.

At last convulsion brought to the already hardening surface only his enormous horn thickly coated with the viscid fluid. All became rock in time, and of the life before the cataclysm there was no witness but this huge monocerous monument.

Millenniums file by and the waste places are redeemed. Seismic upheavals shatter the great plateau, erosion and disintegration play a potent part, forests and rivers appear and make a new world to welcome the fauna of a new age. Men come at last—men who fill the valleys with fields of grain, torture the bowels of the earth in search for precious metals, spread towns in mountain parks, and cast a tenuous path of steel across the mountain ranges. But ever the towering monolith defies them, keeping its lofty heights unsoiled by human touch.

"Lizard Head . . . is a column with nearly vertical walls on all sides, rising nearly three hundred feet above its platform. Its summit is inaccessible, and the reason for its preservation is not evident. At the base it is a bedded mass of andesitic breccia . . . and a horizontal banding is visible far up on its walls, although a vertical fissuring renders this obscure in many places. It is possible that there is here a rounded or oval neck of massive rock . . . which has indurated the surrounding tuffs, so that the core is concealed by a shell of this character."

This curious rocky "Head" is an outcropping at the highest possible point of a long semicircular ridge that forms the eastern portion of the Mt. Wilson group. Geologically this majestic group is but an offshoot or outlier of the San Juan Mountains, but like several other spurs in the Colorado Rockies, it surpasses the main range in ruggedness and alpine dignity and beauty.

Besides the unique Lizard Head, with which we are here concerned, it contains (to mention only the highest peaks) Gladstone Peak (over 13,800 feet), Wilson Peak (14,026 feet) and Mt. Wilson itself (14,250 feet); the last is the fourteenth peak in a State that boasts forty-two peaks over 14,000 feet in height and (to quote from a Forest Service scribe) "offers a difficult and in part a dangerous climb, but affords one of the most beautiful views obtainable in the southern part of the State."

The group as a whole is isolated from the mass of the volcanic complex of the San Juan region by the deep erosion of the San Miguel river, which flows northward into the Gunnison, and the Rio Dolores, which flows in the opposite direction.

The government geologist had said the Lizard Head was inaccessible, and the Forest Service pamphlet corroborated him: "The sheer rock face of Lizard Head Peak (13,156 feet) has never yet been climbed by man."

The Forest Supervisor at Durango wrote in response to my inquiry: "It is my understanding that the Lizard Head has never been scaled." Finally, after taking three weeks to get "reliable information," Mr. Richard R. Thompson, the Forest Ranger at Rico (which is the nearest Ranger Station to the Lizard Head), replied: "It is said that Lizard Head has never been climbed, and I believe that it is unclimbable from either face." "Inaccessible" and "unclimbable" are strong words, and are like a red rag to the enthusiastic alpinist; so, when, with Barton Hoag of Colorado Springs, I planned three weeks of camping and climbing in the San Juan, it is hardly necessary to say the Lizard Head was an objective.

From our first peak, the Uncompahgre, loftiest of the San Juan region (14,306 feet), we sought it eagerly with our powerful glasses, and picking it out with difficulty in the early morning mist across thirty-five miles of the most tangled confusion of mountains in Colorado, let our eyes rest long upon it, in earnest anticipation of what it held in store for us. We had several glimpses of it as we gradually worked closer, from the highest summits of the Lake Fork section of the San Juan proper, and from the Needle Mountains south of Silverton. Finally, from the favored summit of Mt. Sneffles (the finest view in the San Juan), we gazed admiringly upon the slender shaft of rock only fifteen miles away, and wondered if we were destined to stand upon its top.

Our course lay southwest along the sheep driveway for a mile and a half, and then turned off on a trail to the right which brought us to Slate Creek for lunch, for we had not got started till 11:10. So far there was practically no climbing, but now the trail swung to the north and headed for the saddle (11,800 feet) between Gladstone and the Lizard Head, and in the next four and a half miles there is an ascent of 1,600 feet. Relaying the packs to the top of the pass, we dropped down rapidly to the treeline in the east branch of Bilk Basin and pitched camp at about 11,300 feet.

This is undoubtedly the best base of operations. It is at the very foot of the Lizard Head ridge and only 1,500 feet below the platform upon which the great rock rests. It can be reached by trail, either from the Lizard Head station as we came (about eight and a half miles), or from the railway crossing opposite the Belt ranch in the San Miguel valley.

The latter route climbs over the north shoulder of Sunshine Mountain and ascends Bilk Creek; it is shorter than the route we took by perhaps two miles, but involves a climb of 2,600 feet instead of 1,600, and the long stretch in the valley below the camp is very steep indeed for heavy packs. One would have to go a considerable distance from the trail to find both wood and water to the southwest of the Head, and there is no trail at all up Wilson Creek to the east.

The camp in Bilk Basin is also favorably situated for attacking Wilson Peak, Gladstone, and Mt. Wilson. It would be difficult to find a more beautiful site. Pitched on the high east bank of a roaring creek, it looks out from the shelter of tall Engelmanns upon the thick green spruce carpet of the lower Basin, from which the long brown slope of Wilson Peak stretches impressively into the western sky. Farther to the left stands Gladstone's rocky cone, the jagged eastern ridge of which cuts off from view the snowy heights of Mt. Wilson.

For two days we kept close to our tarp lean-to, forced to remain inactive by the unkind weather. The morning of the third was cloudy, but it started to clear after breakfast, and, resolved to let no opportunity escape, we hurriedly packed a lunch and set out for the ridge. An Indian boy who was herding 1,500 sheep over in the West Basin had dropped in for a chat after breakfast, and we told him as we packed that we were going to climb the Lizard Head. He evidently thought we were "ragging" him and was highly amused. If he had believed we were seriously planning such an attempt, doubtless he would have set us down as lunatics.

It sits astride the narrow ridge, in outline very like a rough, Cyclopean arrowhead with shallow notch and somewhat shattered tip. The picture taken from this point shows all of the west face and part of the east as well, for the rock narrows to the north, and the photograph is taken from west of north. Consequently the base appears thicker than it is.

Nor is the apparent height the true one; for, as can be seen from other pictures, the summit is distinctly farther from an observer on this ridge than is the base. According to the geologist quoted above, the top is practically 300 feet above the ridge. The U.S.G.S. map would make it nearer 450, and a calculation made by the writer from observations taken on the ridge gives 350 as the height. The last figure is a minimum if one may judge by the ascent, on which our 100-foot alpine rope made a very good tape measure.

The rock is almost as long as it is high, but probably does not exceed 125 feet in thickness at any point. Only when seen from either side (necessarily from a distance) does it to any degree justify its name, and the writer must confess that even then he thinks its resemblance to a saurian's head not over-strong. A striking feature easily seen in the ridge picture and those taken from the west is the slender pinnacle that springs from a small ledge below and to the northwest of the summit; the "Finger" we called it, and it seemed raised in warning as we went along the ridge.

It was apparent when we reached the Head that there was nasty work before us. A rottener mass of rock is inconceivable. The core may still be solid but the "surrounding tuffs" are seeking a lower level in large quantities. This far-advanced disintegration was our greatest obstacle. Absolutely the whole surface of the rock is loose and pebbles rain down from the sides as readily as needles from an aging Christmas tree.

In many places one could with one hand pull down hundreds of pounds of fragments, and occasionally we could hear the crashing of small avalanches that fell without human prompting. In some parts of the San Juan we had run across the rumor that the Lizard Head or a large part thereof had fallen off a year or two ago; but though the ridge is covered with the detritus of the ages, there is no evidence of a recent catastrophe of any magnitude. However, it is more than probable that large masses plunge down to the long talus slopes from time to time.

We saw at a glance that the east face was out of the question; it is an almost sheer drop from near the summit of the Head to far below the level of the ridge on which we stood. And the north edge was nearly as impossible—its inclination measured 85 degrees. Working along the western side we reached the other end, which is so broad it might be called a face. A peek around the southeast corner confirmed us in our opinion that the east face will not be climbed till man has learned how to defy the law of gravity.

There were a couple of spots along the west face that seemed worth trying as a last resort, but from below they looked like rather a forlorn hope, and after our later experience on the rock it was clear that there would have been little chance of success by any such route. Seen from the pass to the west three days before, the south end had appeared to be the most feasible line of attack, but a closer inspec-

tion showed that there were no holds for more than
a few feet, except in a couple of cracks near the
southwest corner. We roped up and I tried them
both, getting perhaps seventy-five feet in the first
and hardly twenty-five feet in the second when
forced to retreat.

Then we went around the corner and tried the
first promising crack on the west side. This proved
the beginning of a feasible route, so I will try to
describe it carefully, following my diary notes quite
closely. It was about 12:00 when I began this third
attack. Hoag sought shelter around the corner, for
each movement that I made sent down a rattling
shower of stones. Needless to say, every hand- and
foothold had to be tested with the utmost thorough-
ness. Most of the enticing small holds, crumbled at a
touch and large masses of the loosely compacted
pebbles would topple dangerously at a slight pull.

As we topped the ridge the north end of the massive rock burst full upon us with startling suddenness.
The first fifteen or twenty feet was a rather open
stretch, practically vertical and with exiguous holds
about the size of a thimble that at once forced me to
put off my leather gloves. When rock is treacherous
and small firm holds are scarce—and important—
even fingernails may be of use. But soon the crack
deepened and narrowed, and resorting to the back-
and-knee method I felt much more secure. This
cross-bracing became easier as I ascended, but I

sought in vain a secure place to wait for my companion to come up to me.

Grateful indeed I was for the extra length of this rope that had been obtained originally for four-party climbing. With the eighty foot rope that is recommended by Abraham the great English alpinist, I should have been forced to await Hoag in a very wearying cross-braced position, and after he had reached me he would have had to take the same position and protect himself as best he could from the unavoidable hail of stone caused by my further ascent.

At ninety feet I climbed out on a small ledge to the right and found fair standing and two reassuring hand-holds, but, alas! no belaying-pin. Working upwards and into the crack again I went on, pulling Hoag from his shelter to give a few feet more, until, literally at the end of my rope, I found an anchor, safe and secure though rather awkward for the operator. With one foot on a ledge three inches wide and seven or eight inches long, the other swinging in mid-air, the right hand hooked over a small sharp rock at arm's length overhead and the left free to manipulate the rope over a small point about shoulder high, I called "Come on."

The first steep pitch gave a good deal of trouble, as it had to me, but once in the crack, Hoag soon reached the ninety foot ledge and prepared to make himself comfortable. This first one hundred foot section averaged about eighty degrees in inclination, and the lowest pitch and one just under the Hoag ledge were practically perpendicular.

Above me the main crack was quite impossible, and the nose upon the right no less so. A small crack, hardly large enough to thrust one's hand in, branched off to the left across a more open stretch of rock discouragingly steep and smooth. Hoag, who was carrying the rucksack, tied three spikes into the rope and I pulled them up—long, thick spikes, somewhat like those used for steps on telegraph poles. Driving one in the crack about waist high to step upon, I squirmed my way up an eight-foot wall where even the slight friction of my clothes on the almost vertical rock was welcome aid, for there were hand-holds only for the fingertips.

An easier slope succeeded this, but twenty feet farther on there was another pitch that went straight up and ended in a slightly overhanging brow. This delayed progress for some time, but with the aid of another spike and a long cross-brace that stretched me to the limit I finally pulled over and to my great relief found myself on an easier grade (probably about seventy-five degrees). The temptation was to hurry, but the loose rock was especially treacherous and I restrained myself.

At the head of this stretch and once again at the end of my rope, I reached a little platform roughly three feet wide and five feet long and fairly level. A fine anchor rock stood two feet high at its edge, and belaying the rope around this I called for Hoag to join me. It was a chilly wait, for my second bonne bouche gave him quite a bit of trouble with its scarcity of holds and the embarrassing brow that called for very delicate adjustment of one's balance in mid-air; and I had plenty of time to realize he must have well nigh congealed on his narrow ledge while I was struggling with these difficulties for the first time.

This was his introduction to prime rock climbing, and I was more than pleased with his patience, skill and caution. He reached the anchorage in fine fettle, and we pushed on at once.

A six-foot wall confronted us. Easily but gingerly we climbed around and up over its right nose, and found ourselves on a large shelf sloping to the south at perhaps thirty degrees, and cut into north and south by a couple of narrow rock gullies that evidently led to cracks on the south end of the Head. Carefully we worked to the left, gaining about fifty feet in altitude before coming up against the sheer, smooth cliff at the head of the shelf. It looked decidedly dubious at first. There were cracks higher up on the wall, but they all ran out eight or ten feet above the base.

Any route would be slow at best, and we could not see what impossibilities awaited us at the top. The summit of the Head was somewhere to the north— but how far and how much higher and behind what barricades? These were pertinent questions, for the afternoon was waning rapidly.

Finally I decided to try to reach a crack that lay near the south end of the wall and appeared to lead through to the arete above. The first eight or nine feet was an overhanging pocket or alcove, and above this the wall was vertical and unbroken save for the narrow end of the crack to which we aspired. It was a difficult problem—one of the four real pieces de resistance of the whole climb.

Standing on Hoag's shoulders, I proved all things within reach for what must have seemed an interminable time to him. At last I found holds at arm's length, but it was a strenuous pull to reach the crack. Equally strenuous it was, though not difficult technically, to wriggle up the narrow cleft with a very crowded back-and-knee cross-brace. This was the safest stretch of the day, and the hardest physical work.

At the extreme limit of the rope I reached a large, safe anchor rock at the south end of the summit arete, and saw that we had won. Shouting down the glad tidings, I told Hoag to come on. He had no shoulders to support him but a rope above, and after he was over the alcove all went well.

From this last anchor rock there is an easy ascent northwards along a fairly sharp ridge of loose rock, across a small gap where one gets a sensational view down the sheer east cliffs, and finally a careful climb over a few large rocks to the top, which is perhaps fifty feet above the anchor rock. The situation was not without its thrills. The actual summit is quite small and the rocks are ready to slide off on every side. There was no sign that anyone had been before us.

We built a cairn as large as we could find support for, and placed at its foot a Prince Albert tobacco can containing a slip of paper with the usual data. Unfortunately the terrain did not permit a good picture of the top, but each of us snapped the other precariously balanced near the cairn.

The sun was too low by this time to expect good results, but we tried to get some photographic record of the intricate jumble of mountains along the eastern skyline and of the magnificent Wilson group to the west. The lonesome Lizard Head is an ideal position for both views. Also we got a spectacular close-up of the fifteen-foot Finger, which looked as if it were so far gone that the slightest push would topple it from its resting place.

We agreed that a million dollars would not tempt us to its top—for riches are of this world, not the next. Incidentally, it would be a painstaking feat to reach its base.

We had arrived at 4:25, and a half-hour escaped before we could bring ourselves to leave. The return route was the same for we had no time to waste on very dubious experiments. Hoag made good speed down the first crack. I drove in a spike and looped the rope around it to secure me for the first few feet, then shook it off, wriggled down easily to the alcove, and jumped.

The second hundred was our *bete noire*. Hoag went down to his old ledge, leaning heavily on the rope and moving an inch at a time down the two spiked walls. There he untied the rope and prepared for as comfortable a sojourn as possible.

Looping the rope at its middle around the big anchor rock, I went down to the first spike, grateful indeed for the rope when I dropped over the projecting brow. It was a ticklish task to get past this *mauvais pas*, and I wondered again and again how I had ever ascended it without a rope, being quite certain I would not come down it ropeless for a good deal. My plan was to pull the loose end of the rope around the rock, loop it again over the spike to which I now clung and then drop on down to the first anchor of the day.

But, alas, the rope would not come. I shook it violently to loosen it—and something else came. A stone as large as my fist suddenly shot off the brow and landed squarely on the top of my head. I have a thick head of hair, and fortunately, contrary to my usual practice, I was wearing a heavy hat. Even so, the scalp was broken (as I found later), and I was nearly knocked from my very insecure position. I felt light-headed and tied closely to the spike for a few minutes, to make sure that I could find myself when wanted.

Hoag had suffered too; a small rock ricochetted and, traveling at good speed, smote him on the back of the head as he bowed to protect his face against the flying pebbles. Luckily he was well braced on the ledge, and his hands were clenched and cramped over good holds. But it was a close shave, for he saw many stars and carried a bump like a large walnut for several days to come.

Worst of all, the rope could not be budged. I climbed up, readjusted it and tried again, but to no purpose. It was not jammed, but there was enough friction on the rough surface of the big rock and on the slope and brow to resist all the pull I could exert. Up again I went and reconnoitred. There was no other possible anchor. I scouted the gullies leading to the south end cracks—to no avail.

Hoag and I held a long-distance consultation. I made one more round-trip and profited nothing. It was enough; the rope must go the way of so many ropes on Chamonix aiguilles. I tied the end to the stubborn anchor and went down to my old ledge near Hoag. He used the last few feet to steady him into the crack, let go, and worked slowly toward the ground.

The last pitch balked him for some time. The small holds that had assisted us up were undiscoverable. Suddenly he slipped and, leaving a section of his pants behind, drifted relentlessly downward till the wall became vertical and then jumped (perhaps fifteen feet) to the rocks below. I followed with more caution, regretfully saying goodbye to the rope that had served me for five good seasons.

All went well till the holds got scarce. It was too dark now to see what was below me on the cliff and I did not care to risk a jump and possibly a sprained ankle unless I had to. So I let down a long string for the folding lantern that we had left behind at noontide, and by its light slowly picked my way down to the ground.

It was a quarter to nine, and the sandwiches and raisins from the second rucksack were as good as a five-course dinner at the Ritz. There was a bright moon now, just at the full, and, once out of the Head's huge shadow, we had easy going over the talus slopes and snow-filled ravines to camp. Getting a hot supper and exchanging gratified reminiscences of the climb brought midnight before we sought our blankets.

Our Indian friend dropped in next morning as we were setting out for Wilson Peak and Mt. Wilson, and we told him we had stood upon Lizard Head. He grinned as pleasantly and as incredulously as ever. It was still a good joke, anyway.

Sources

"The Ascent of Mount Ventoux" from *Canzoniere*
by Francesco Petrarch, 1336.

"Jacques Balmat or The first Ascent of Mont Blanc:
A True Story" from *Jacques Balmat or The First
Ascent of Mont Blanc: A True Story*, T. Louis
Oxley, 1881.

"Mount Katahdin" from *Maine Woods*, Henry David
Thoreau, 1864.

"The Schreckhorn" from *The Playground of Europe*,
by Leslie Stephen, 1895.

"The First Ascent of the Matterhorn" from *Scrambles Amongst the Alps*, by Edward Whymper,
1900.

"The Descent of the Matterhorn" from *Scrambles
Amongst the Alps*, by Edward Whymper, 1900.

"The Ascent of Mount Takhoma [Mount Rainier]"
from *Atlantic Monthly*, by General Hazard
Stevens, November 1876.